ESTATE PLANNING MADE SIMPLE

Riley G. Foster

INTRODUCTION

Welcome to a comprehensive journey into the world of estate planning. This book is designed to guide you through the intricacies of preparing for the future, ensuring your assets are managed and distributed according to your wishes, and providing for your loved ones after you're gone.

The realm of estate planning can often seem shrouded in complexity, with its own language and myriad legal considerations. Whether you are starting your first job, welcoming a new family member, or looking ahead to retirement, the strategies and knowledge contained within these pages will empower you to take control of your estate.

We begin with the essentials, demystifying estate planning and emphasizing its importance for everyone—not just the wealthy. Through real-life examples, we'll dispel common misconceptions and lay the foundation for understanding why proactive planning is crucial.

Part II delves into crafting your personalized estate plan. From asset inventories to writing your will, establishing trusts, and selecting powers of attorney, I'll provide you with a checklist and tools for laying a solid foundation. We'll address the unique challenges of blended families and the nuances they bring to estate planning.

As you progress to Part III, we tackle the topic of tax planning. We dissect estate taxes, gift taxes, and other state-level considerations, furnishing you with strategies to minimize your tax liabilities and maximize the benefits for your beneficiaries.

Finally, Part IV explores the role of life insurance in estate planning. You'll learn how different policies can offer both protection and strategic benefits, and how advanced tools like Irrevocable Life Insurance Trusts can play a pivotal role in your estate plan.

Throughout the book, I ensure that complex terms are well explained within each context they appear. However, for quick reference or further clarification, you will find a detailed glossary at the end of this book. This comprehensive glossary serves as a resource to consult for definitions of terms used throughout our discussion.

Whether you're new to estate planning or looking to update an existing plan, this book is your ally. With practical advice, step-by-step guides, and expert insights, I aim to provide you with the knowledge and confidence to ensure your estate is a lasting testament to your life and values.

Before we commence, remember to secure your future by obtaining the bonuses:

Scan the QR Code below to access the bonuses:

In addition, you can get the opportunity to become a part of our exclusive ARC team. As a member, you'll have the chance to receive early releases of new books, provide feedback, and help shape the future publications. This is a wonderful opportunity for avid readers and enthusiasts in the field to engage more deeply with our content and contribute to the community. Scan the QR code below and get access to the ARC team.

Also, if you will enjoy the book, please consider leaving a review. Your feedback is crucial in helping others discover the resources they need for their estate planning, and it assists me in continually providing better content.

PART I: THE ESSENTIALS OF ESTATE PLANNING

Understanding Estate Planning: The Basics and Importance for Everyone

Estate planning is an essential process that involves preparing for the transfer of a person's wealth and assets after their death. At its core, estate planning is about ensuring that your wishes are respected, your family is protected, and your financial goals are met, even when you're no longer around to oversee them. This process is not just for the wealthy; it's a crucial step for anyone who wants to safeguard their assets and provide for their loved ones.

Why Everyone Needs Estate Planning

Many people mistakenly believe that estate planning is only for the affluent. However, almost everyone has an estate, which is simply the sum total of everything you own. Your estate might include your home, car, other real estate, checking and savings accounts, investments, life insurance, furniture, and personal possessions. No matter how large or small, your estate represents your life's work and legacy. Estate planning is vital for several reasons:

1. **Asset Distribution**: It allows you to control who receives your assets after your death, ensuring that your belongings go to the individuals or organizations you choose.

2. **Family Protection**: It helps protect the financial stability and well-being of your loved ones, preventing unnecessary stress during an already difficult time.

3. **Legal Costs and Delays**: Proper estate planning can significantly reduce the legal costs, taxes, and delays often associated with transferring assets to heirs.

4. **Medical Decisions**: It enables you to make critical decisions about your medical care in case you become incapacitated, ensuring that your health care preferences are honored.

5. **Minimizing Family Conflict**: One of the less discussed, yet equally important benefits of estate planning, is its role in minimizing potential conflicts among family members. Without clear directives on how assets should be distributed, disputes can arise, leading to strained relationships and even prolonged legal battles. Estate planning allows you to specify your wishes clearly, reducing the chances of misunderstanding or disagreement among your heirs.

6. **Guardianship for Minor Children**: If you have minor children, estate planning becomes even more critical. In your will, you can designate a guardian for your children in the event of your death, ensuring they are cared for by someone you trust. Without such a designation, the

court will decide who will take care of your children, which might not align with your preferences.

7. **Charitable Contributions**: Estate planning also offers an opportunity to leave a lasting legacy through charitable giving. You can specify portions of your estate to go towards charities or causes you are passionate about. This not only helps the organizations you support but can also provide tax benefits to your estate.

8. **Business Continuity**: For business owners, estate planning is crucial for outlining what happens to your business after you're gone. A well-crafted estate plan can ensure the smooth transition of business ownership, thereby safeguarding your employees' jobs and the enterprise you've built.

9. **Privacy Protection**: Many people don't realize that wills become public record once they are probated. If privacy is a concern, a properly structured trust can keep your affairs out of the public eye. Trusts allow for the private and efficient transfer of assets, ensuring your financial matters remain confidential.

10. **Avoiding Probate**: Perhaps one of the most significant advantages of estate planning, particularly through the establishment of a trust, is avoiding probate. Probate can be a lengthy, public, and expensive process. Assets held in a trust can bypass probate entirely, allowing for a more efficient and private transfer of your estate.

11. **Peace of Mind**: Finally, having a comprehensive estate plan in place gives peace of mind. Knowing that you have taken steps to secure your legacy and protect your loved ones can alleviate worries about the future. Estate planning allows you to face life's uncertainties with confidence, knowing that your wishes will be respected and your loved ones cared for.

Key Components of Estate Planning

1. **Will**: A legal document that outlines how you want your assets distributed after your death. It also allows you to name guardians for any minor children.

2. **Trust**: A legal arrangement through which a trustee holds and manages assets on behalf of beneficiaries. Trusts can help avoid probate, reduce estate taxes, and provide more control over asset distribution.

3. **Power of Attorney**: A legal document that grants someone you trust the authority to make decisions on your behalf in the event that you're unable to do so. This can cover both financial and health care decisions.

4. **Beneficiary Designations**: Many financial accounts and life insurance policies allow you to specify who will receive the assets in those accounts upon your death, bypassing the will and probate process.

5. **Health Care Directives**: These include a living will and a health care power of attorney, allowing you to outline your wishes for medical treatment and appoint someone to make health care decisions if you're unable to communicate.

The Importance of Proactive Planning

Estate planning is often perceived as a task for the distant future, a necessary step to be taken when the time seems right. However, the essence and true value of estate planning reside in its proactive approach. By initiating the estate planning process now, you're not just preparing for the inevitable; you're ensuring that your choices are respected, your family's future is secure, and your legacy is crafted precisely as you envision. This approach underscores the critical importance of proactive planning in estate management, offering a tangible way to protect your loved ones and preserve your legacy with intention and foresight.

Contrary to common belief, estate planning is not an endeavor reserved for the later stages of life or the exceedingly wealthy. Beginning the process early, even with a basic plan, lays the groundwork for a more detailed and complex strategy as your circumstances and financial landscape change. Starting sooner rather than later ensures you are well-prepared for life's unpredictable moments, offering invaluable peace of mind to both you and your family.

The Cautionary Tales of Aretha Franklin, Sonny Bono, and Prince

The narratives of Aretha Franklin, Sonny Bono, and Prince serve as compelling testament to the critical importance of proactive estate planning. Each of these iconic figures left behind a legacy marred by the absence of a clear, legally recognized will, leading to prolonged legal disputes, diminished estate values, and public scrutiny that could have been mitigated with proper planning.

Aretha Franklin: The Queen of Soul's Dissonant Finale

When Aretha Franklin passed away in 2018, she left behind not just a towering musical legacy but also a tangled legal predicament that spotlighted the pitfalls of inadequate estate planning. Despite her significant assets and a complex family situation, Franklin died without a formal will. In the months following her death, multiple handwritten documents were discovered in her home, leading to disputes among her four sons about which document, if any, represented her true final wishes. The ensuing legal battle, drawn out over years, underscored the challenges and uncertainties that can arise when clear directives are not laid out in a legally binding document.

Sonny Bono: An Unscripted Exit

Sonny Bono's sudden death in a skiing accident in 1998 left his estate in limbo, as he had not prepared a will. His widow, Mary Bono, faced immediate challenges in seeking to administer his estate, compounded by claims from an ex-wife for unpaid alimony and child support and a surprise paternity claim. The lack of a will meant that the distribution of Bono's assets would be subject to state law and court discretion, igniting a complex legal struggle that highlighted the critical need for explicit estate planning, regardless of one's age or the seeming stability of one's personal circumstances.

Prince: The Legend Without a Will

The death of Prince in 2016 sent shockwaves not only through the music world but also through legal circles, as it was revealed that he had no will. Despite an estate estimated at hundreds of millions of dollars, including unreleased music and rights to his existing works, Prince's lack of estate planning initiated a complex and public probate process. With numerous individuals coming forward claiming to be heirs, the court had to step in to determine the rightful beneficiaries. This not only prolonged the distribution of his assets but also incurred substantial legal costs, significantly reducing the estate's value.

Reflections on Their Stories

The stories of Franklin, Bono, and Prince illustrate not only the universal need for estate planning but also the unique challenges that can arise from fame and public life. Their experiences highlight several key points:

- **The Universality of Estate Planning Needs**: Regardless of one's level of wealth or public profile, everyone stands to benefit from clear, legally sound estate planning.
- **The Potential for Dispute Among Heirs**: The absence of a will can lead to family disputes, as seen in Franklin's case, where the discovery of multiple wills led to uncertainty and legal wrangling among her sons.
- **The Importance of a Formal Will**: All three stories demonstrate the potential complications of dying intestate (without a will), from unresolved claims against the estate to uncertainty about the distribution of assets.
- **The Public Nature of Probate**: Without a will to direct the private distribution of their estates, the probate processes for these celebrities became public spectacles, offering a cautionary tale about the loss of privacy that can accompany intestate succession.

The Probate Process

Probate is a legal procedure through which a deceased person's estate is properly distributed to heirs and designated beneficiaries and any debt owed to creditors is paid off. It involves validating the deceased's will, if one exists, and is often supervised by a probate court. While the process is generally standardized, specific laws and requirements can vary significantly from one jurisdiction to another. Understanding the steps involved can demystify what is often perceived as a daunting process.

1. Filing a Petition and Notifying Heirs and Beneficiaries

The probate process begins with the filing of a petition with the probate court to either admit the will to probate and appoint the executor or, if there is no will, appoint an estate administrator. This step involves notifying all potential heirs, beneficiaries, and sometimes creditors about the start of the probate process, often through direct notice and sometimes through newspaper publication.

2. Inventorying the Deceased's Assets

One of the executor's or administrator's first duties is to identify and take inventory of the deceased's assets. This includes both tangible and intangible assets. The inventory offers a comprehensive snapshot of what the estate comprises and is used to determine the estate's value for tax purposes and distribution to beneficiaries.

3. Appraising the Estate's Assets

After inventorying the assets, an appraisal may be necessary to determine their current value. Appraisals are particularly important for assets whose values can fluctuate, such as real estate, stocks, and personal items like art or jewelry. This step is crucial for accurately managing the estate and ensuring fair distribution.

4. Paying the Estate's Debts and Taxes

Before distributing assets to beneficiaries, the executor or administrator must settle any outstanding debts owed by the estate. This may include funeral expenses, outstanding loans, and personal debts. Additionally, the estate may owe state and/or federal estate taxes, which must be calculated and paid out of the estate's assets.

5. Legal Title Transfer and Asset Distribution

Once debts and taxes are settled, the remaining assets can be distributed to the beneficiaries as outlined in the will or, if there's no will, according to state intestacy laws. This often involves transferring the legal title of assets such as real estate and vehicles to the new owners and distributing funds from bank and investment accounts.

6. Closing the Estate

The final step in the probate process is to close the estate. This involves preparing and filing a final accounting that details all income to the estate, bills paid, and distributions to beneficiaries. Once approved by the court, the executor or administrator will file a petition for discharge, releasing them from their duties.

The probate process can be complex and time-consuming, often lasting several months to a few years, depending on the estate's size, the clarity of the will, and the jurisdiction's specific requirements. While many seek to avoid probate through estate planning tools like living trusts, it remains a common legal procedure for settling estates. Understanding probate's intricacies can help individuals better prepare their estate plans and navigate the process more effectively when the time comes. Consulting with an estate planning attorney can give valuable guidance and help simplify this process, ensuring a smoother transition for all involved.

Why to Avoid Probate

While probate is a standard legal procedure designed to settle a deceased person's estate, many individuals opt to structure their estate plans to avoid or minimize the probate process. There are several compelling reasons to consider strategies that circumvent probate, each rooted in the desire to simplify the distribution of one's assets and reduce the burden on surviving family members.

1. Time-Consuming Process

Probate can be a lengthy process, often stretching over several months to several years, depending on the complexity of the estate, the clarity of the will (if one exists), and the specific probate laws of the jurisdiction. During this time, beneficiaries may have limited access to the estate's assets, which can be particularly challenging if they rely on those assets for financial support.

2. Financial Costs

Probate incurs various costs, including court fees, legal fees, executor fees, and appraisal costs, which are paid out of the estate's assets. This can significantly reduce the amount of inheritance that passes to the beneficiaries. By avoiding probate, you can help ensure that a larger portion of your estate goes directly to your loved ones.

3. Loss of Privacy

Probate is a public process. Documents filed in probate court, including the deceased's will and the inventory of their assets, become part of the public record. This lack of privacy can be unsettling as sensitive information about the value and distribution of your estate becomes accessible to anyone who seeks it.

4. Potential for Family Conflict

The probate process can sometimes exacerbate existing family tensions. Disputes over asset distribution or the interpretation of the deceased's wishes can lead to contentious legal battles among heirs and beneficiaries. These disputes not only prolong the probate process but can also cause lasting rifts within families.

5. Complications with Multiple Jurisdictions

For estates that include assets in multiple states or countries, probate can become even more complicated. Each jurisdiction may require a separate probate proceeding, known as ancillary probate, further complicating the settlement process and increasing costs and delays.

Strategies to Avoid Probate

Thankfully, several estate planning tools and strategies can help avoid or minimize the impact of probate:

- **Living Trusts**: Placing assets in a revocable living trust allows those assets to bypass probate, facilitating a quicker and private transfer to beneficiaries.
- **Joint Ownership**: Assets owned jointly with rights of survivorship automatically pass to the surviving owner without going through probate.
- **Payable-On-Death and Transfer-On-Death Accounts**: Designating beneficiaries on bank accounts, investment accounts, and even real estate can allow these assets to transfer directly to beneficiaries upon death.
- **Gifting**: Gifting assets during your lifetime can reduce the size of your estate that is subject to probate, although this strategy may have tax implications.

Avoiding probate is a common goal in estate planning, motivated by the desire to streamline the transfer of assets, maintain privacy, reduce costs, and minimize potential conflicts among beneficiaries. By carefully selecting and implementing the appropriate estate planning tools, you can ensure a smoother and more efficient transition of your assets to your loved ones, reflecting your choices and sparing them unnecessary complications during a difficult time. As with all aspects of estate planning, consulting with a professional can provide tailored advice to best achieve your objectives.

PART II: CRAFTING YOUR ESTATE PLAN

Estate Planning Checklist - Laying the Foundation

Before we dive deep into the intricacies of structuring your estate plan, it's vital to start with a clear roadmap. Together we'll explore an exhaustive checklist that acts as your preliminary guide to laying the groundwork for a robust estate plan. This checklist is designed to be your first step in the journey of estate planning, ensuring you have a solid foundation before exploring the more detailed aspects of crafting your plan. Whether your estate is straightforward or involves more complex considerations, this checklist is an indispensable starting point for safeguarding your legacy and ensuring your loved ones are well cared for according to your wishes.

Essential Documents

- **Last Will and Testament**: Confirms how you want to distribute your assets, appoint guardians for minor children, and designate an executor.
- **Living Trust**: Avoids probate by allowing you to appoint a trustee to manage your assets for the benefit of your beneficiaries.
- **Financial Power of Attorney**: Designates an individual to handle your financial affairs should you become incapacitated.
- **Healthcare Power of Attorney**: Appoints someone to make medical decisions on your behalf if you're unable to do so.
- **Living Will**: Specifies your wishes regarding end-of-life medical care.
- **Beneficiary Designations**: Ensures that accounts like life insurance, retirement plans, and bank accounts pass directly to your chosen beneficiaries.

Assets and Beneficiaries

- **Inventory of Assets**: Compile a detailed list of all your assets, including real estate, bank accounts, investments, personal property, and digital assets.
- **Review Beneficiary Designations**: Regularly update beneficiaries for life insurance policies, retirement accounts, and any other accounts with designated beneficiaries.
- **Special Considerations for Digital Assets**: Include instructions for managing digital assets such as social media accounts, digital wallets, and online businesses.

Family Needs and Special Provisions

- **Guardianship for Minor Children**: Clearly state your choice of guardian for your minor children in your will to ensure they're cared for by someone you trust.

- **Care Plans for Dependents with Special Needs**: Consider a special needs trust to provide for dependents without affecting their eligibility for government assistance.
- **Instructions for Pets**: Include arrangements for the care of your pets, possibly through a pet trust.

Review and Update

- **Regular Review**: Estate plans should not be static. Review and update your estate plan regularly, especially after major life events like marriage, divorce, birth of a child, or significant changes in your financial situation.
- **Consult Professionals**: Engage with estate planning attorneys, financial advisors, and tax professionals to ensure your plan is legally sound and meets your objectives.

Storage and Communication

- **Secure Storage**: Keep your original estate planning documents in a secure, fireproof location. Inform your executor, trustees, or a trusted family member of the location.
- **Provide Copies to Relevant Parties**: Give copies of relevant documents to your executor, powers of attorney, and healthcare proxy.
- **Digital Access**: If applicable, provide instructions for accessing digital assets, including a list of accounts, passwords, and any other necessary information, stored securely and separately from other estate documents.

Completing this estate planning checklist is a significant step toward ensuring your wishes are honored and your loved ones are provided for in the manner you intend. By methodically addressing each item on the checklist, you can create a comprehensive estate plan that reflects your values, protects your assets, and offers peace of mind. Remember, estate planning is an ongoing process that requires attention and updates as your life and laws change.

Inventory and Asset Allocation

Understanding Asset Valuation and Its Importance in Estate Planning

Asset valuation is a fundamental aspect of estate planning, serving as the bedrock for informed decision-making and effective estate management. It involves determining the current worth of your assets, a process that influences everything from tax liabilities to how assets are allocated among heirs. Let's explore the significance of asset valuation in estate planning, outlining key considerations and methodologies for accurately assessing the value of different types of assets.

The Role of Asset Valuation in Estate Planning

Valuing your assets accurately is crucial for several reasons:

- **Equitable Distribution**: Asset valuation ensures that your estate is distributed according to your liking and in a fair manner among your heirs, especially when specific assets are bequeathed to particular individuals.
- **Tax Implications**: The total value of your estate impacts estate taxes. Understanding the value of your assets can help in planning strategies to minimize tax liabilities.
- **Financial Planning**: Valuation informs financial planning for your estate, including decisions about gifting, setting up trusts, and other mechanisms to manage the estate's future.

Understanding What Constitutes Your Assets

Assets can broadly be categorized into two types: tangible and intangible.

- **Tangible Assets** are physical items such as real estate properties, vehicles, jewelry, artwork, collectibles, and household items.
- **Intangible Assets** include financial accounts (savings, checking, retirement accounts), stocks and bonds, life insurance policies, and digital assets like online accounts or cryptocurrency.

Key Considerations in Asset Valuation

- **Frequency of Valuation**: Asset values can fluctuate over time due to market conditions, depreciation, and other factors. Regular revaluation ensures that your estate plan reflects the most current asset values.
- **Professional Assistance**: For many assets, particularly real estate, businesses, and high-value personal property, professional appraisals are recommended to ensure accurate valuations.
- **Documentation**: Keep detailed records of valuations and appraisals, including the basis for valuation and any assumptions made. This documentation is crucial for estate planning purposes and can be vital in the event of disputes or audits.
- **Market Conditions**: Understanding the current market conditions and how they affect asset values is crucial. Economic downturns, for example, can decrease the value of certain assets, while others may appreciate.

Accurate asset valuation is a cornerstone of effective estate planning, providing a clear picture of your estate's worth and ensuring that your planning objectives can be met. Whether it's for tax planning, equitable distribution, or financial management, understanding the value of your assets—and how that value is determined—is crucial. Engaging with professionals for complex valuations and maintaining up-to-date records of your assets' worth are key steps in safeguarding your estate and ensuring your legacy is managed according to your wishes.

Taking Inventory of Your Assets: A Foundational Step in Estate Planning

Before diving into the specifics of drafting a will or exploring alternatives like trusts, the first essential step in estate planning is to take a comprehensive inventory of your assets. This process lays the groundwork for all subsequent estate planning decisions, providing a clear picture of what constitutes your estate. Here's a guide on how to systematically approach this task.

Step 1: Start with Real Estate

Real estate often represents a significant portion of an individual's assets. For each property you own:

- **Detail the Property Type**: Specify whether it's residential, commercial, land, or another type of real estate.
- **Location**: Include the full address and any identifying details.
- **Ownership Details**: Note whether you own the property outright, jointly, or as part of a trust or business entity.
- **Financial Information**: Document the purchase price, current market value (an appraisal may be necessary), outstanding mortgage or loan balances, and any rental income it generates.
- **Legal Documents**: Reference deeds, mortgage documents, lease agreements, and property tax information.

Step 2: Catalog Personal Property

Personal property can vary widely, from everyday items to valuable collectibles:

- **High-Value Items**: For items like jewelry, art, antiques, or collectibles, list each item separately with descriptions, appraised values, and any certificates of authenticity or appraisals you have.
- **Vehicles**: Include cars, boats, motorcycles, and other vehicles, noting make, model, year, VIN, and current estimated value.
- **General Household Items**: For furniture, electronics, and other general items, group them into categories and provide a general estimate of their total value.

Step 3: List Financial Accounts

Your financial accounts form the backbone of your liquid assets:

- **Bank Accounts**: Document account numbers, the names of financial institutions, and current balances for checking and savings accounts.
- **Investment Accounts**: Include brokerage accounts, mutual funds, stocks, bonds, and any other investments, with account numbers, institutions, and current values.
- **Retirement Accounts**: Detail all retirement accounts like IRAs, 401(k)s, and pensions, noting the account holders, beneficiaries, and current balances.

Step 4: Document Life Insurance and Annuities

Life insurance policies and annuities can significantly impact estate planning:

- **Policy Details**: For each policy, list the policy number, the insurance company, the type of insurance (term, whole life, etc.), the death benefit, and the named beneficiaries.
- **Annuities**: Include similar information for any annuities, focusing on the benefit amount and the beneficiaries.

Step 5: Include Business Interests

If you have business interests, they should be carefully documented:

- **Business Type and Structure**: Note whether it's a sole proprietorship, partnership, LLC, or corporation, and describe your ownership interest.
- **Valuation**: If available, include a current business valuation and how it was determined.
- **Operating Agreements**: Reference any agreements that might affect the transfer of your business interest.

Step 6: Account for Digital Assets

The digital domain is an increasingly important aspect of estate assets:

- **Online Financial Accounts**: List accounts for online banking, investment platforms, and peer-to-peer payment services.
- **Social Media and Email**: Note usernames for personal and professional accounts, considering privacy and legacy preferences.
- **Digital Collections**: Include information about digital libraries, photos, videos, and websites you own.
- **Cryptocurrency**: Document wallets, keys, and the type and amount of cryptocurrency held.

Step 7: Record Loans and Debts

An accurate picture of your estate includes liabilities:

- **Loans and Mortgages**: List all personal and real estate loans, including lender information, balance, and monthly payment.
- **Credit Cards**: Document credit card accounts with outstanding balances.
- **Other Debts**: Include any other debts, such as personal loans from friends or family, with terms and repayment schedules.

Organizing and Maintaining Your Inventory

After gathering this information:

- **Create a Master Document**: Use a spreadsheet or estate planning software to organize the information, making it easy to update.

- **Secure and Accessible Storage**: Store the document in a secure yet accessible place, and let your executor or a trusted family member know where it is.
- **Regular Reviews**: Your asset inventory should be reviewed annually or after significant life events to ensure it remains accurate and reflective of your current situation.

Creating a detailed asset inventory is a critical first step in estate planning. It not only provides a clear overview of what you own but also ensures that your estate plan can be executed according to your choices, laying a strong foundation for the protection and distribution of your legacy.

The Will - Your Estate Planning Cornerstone

The cornerstone of any comprehensive estate plan is the will—a legal testament that ensures your assets are distributed according to your wishes upon your death. A will goes beyond mere asset distribution; it reflects your intentions, provides for your loved ones, and secures the future of minor children under your care. This chapter delves into the critical aspects of a will, underscoring its pivotal role in estate planning.

Defining the Will

A will, or a last will and testament, is a legally binding document that articulates how you desire your assets to be distributed after your passing. It is the voice that speaks on your behalf, detailing who receives your property, whether they are family members, friends, or charitable organizations. Beyond asset distribution, a will offers the unique ability to appoint guardians for any minor children, ensuring they are cared for by individuals you trust in the event of your untimely demise.

The Components of a Will

Understanding the components of a will can empower individuals to make informed decisions about how their assets and responsibilities are handled after their passing. While the specific content of a will can vary based on personal preferences and legal requirements, certain fundamental elements are universally recognized. Here's an in-depth examination of these components:

Introduction and Declaration

The will typically begins with an introduction that identifies the document as your last will and testament. This section includes your full name and residence, affirming your legal age and mental capacity to create the will. It's here you declare your intention for the document to serve as your will, revoking all previous wills and codicils. This declaration sets the legal foundation for the document.

Appointment of an Executor

A crucial component of a will is the appointment of an executor, sometimes known as a personal representative. This individual is entrusted with the responsibility of administering your estate according to the instructions laid out in your will. The executor's duties include gathering and appraising assets, paying debts and taxes, and distributing the remaining assets to the named beneficiaries. Given the significant responsibilities involved, choosing a reliable, organized, and trustworthy executor is paramount.

Specifications for Asset Distribution

Central to a will is the detailed instruction for asset distribution. This section specifies which assets (e.g., real estate, bank accounts, personal property) go to which beneficiaries. You can be as specific or as general as you like, but clarity is key to preventing misunderstandings and ensuring your wishes are executed as intended. For assets of sentimental value or significant worth, detailed descriptions and clear beneficiary designations are especially important.

Guardianship of Minor Children

For parents or legal guardians of minor children, appointing a guardian in the event of their untimely death is perhaps the most emotionally charged decision made in a will. This section outlines who you would want to care for your children, reflecting your trust in their ability to raise your children in a manner you deem fit. Considering the guardian's values, parenting style, and the emotional and financial capacity to take on such a role is critical.

Special Bequests and Legacies

Special bequests or legacies refer to specific items or fixed sums of money left to individuals or organizations. This could include family heirlooms, specific amounts of money to friends or relatives, or donations to charities. Distinguishing these bequests from the general distribution of assets allows you to honor particular relationships and support causes important to you.

Signatures and Witnesses

For a will to be legally valid, it must be signed by you (the testator) in the presence of a specified number of adult witnesses, depending on jurisdictional requirements. These witnesses must also sign the will, attesting to your declaration that the document is your will, made voluntarily and without undue influence. In many jurisdictions, the witnesses cannot be beneficiaries of the will to prevent conflicts of interest.

Optional Components

- **Residuary Clause**: This clause deals with the residue of the estate - anything not specifically mentioned elsewhere in the will. It ensures that any remaining assets are distributed according to your wishes, rather than defaulting to state law.

- **Funeral Instructions**: While not legally binding in many jurisdictions, some wills include preferences for funeral arrangements or the disposition of the body (burial, cremation, etc.). However, because wills are often read after such arrangements are made, it's advisable to communicate these wishes separately to your family or executor.
- **Digital Assets**: Increasingly, wills are including provisions for digital assets, such as social media accounts, online storage, and cryptocurrencies. Specifying how these should be handled can prevent loss of assets and personal histories.

Different Types Of Wills

Understanding the different types of wills can help you make informed decisions about your estate planning. Each type serves unique needs and situations, providing various ways to ensure that your wishes are carried out after your passing. Here are some common types of wills and their distinctive features:

1. Simple Will

A simple will is the most basic form of a will, suitable for individuals with straightforward estate planning needs. It outlines how your assets should be distributed, appoints an executor, and may specify guardians for minor children. Simple wills are best for smaller estates and when you want to leave everything to a few beneficiaries.

2. Testamentary Trust Will

A testamentary trust will establishes one or more trusts upon your death. It offers a higher level of control over the distribution of your assets, allowing you to specify conditions under which beneficiaries can access their inheritance. This type of will is beneficial if you have minor children or want to leave assets to someone who may not manage them wisely.

3. Joint Will

Joint wills are created by two people, typically married couples, who agree to leave their assets to each other. Upon the death of one party, the surviving individual inherits everything, and after the second party's death, the assets are distributed according to the mutual agreement outlined in the will. However, joint wills are irrevocable after the first person dies, which can be restrictive.

4. Living Will

A living will (not to be confused with a living trust) is a document that outlines your wishes regarding medical treatment if you become unable to communicate or make decisions due to illness or incapacity. It often includes your preferences about life-sustaining treatments, pain management, and other end-of-life care options.

5. Pour-Over Will

A pour-over will works in conjunction with a living trust. It specifies that any assets not included in the trust at the time of your death should "pour over" into the trust and be distributed according to its terms. This ensures that all your assets are eventually managed under the trust, even those not initially placed in it.

6. Holographic Will

Holographic wills are handwritten and signed by the testator without the presence of witnesses. While not all jurisdictions recognize holographic wills as valid, they can be a quick way to express your wishes in emergencies. However, because of their informal nature and the potential for challenges, they are generally not recommended as a primary estate planning tool.

7. Nuncupative Will

A nuncupative will is an oral will made in front of witnesses, usually under urgent circumstances where making a written will isn't possible. The validity of nuncupative wills is limited and not recognized in all jurisdictions, primarily due to the difficulty in verifying the testator's wishes and the potential for disputes.

Choosing the right type of will depends on your specific circumstances, assets, and how you would like to distribute them. While some individuals may find a simple will sufficient, others may require more complex arrangements, like testamentary trusts or pour-over wills, to meet their estate planning goals. Consulting with an estate planning attorney can help you understand the options available in your jurisdiction and select the type of will that best suits your needs, ensuring that your legacy is protected and your wishes are honored.

A Step-by-Step Guide to Writing Your Will

Creating a will is a fundamental aspect of estate planning, ensuring that your assets are distributed according to your wishes upon your death. While the thought of drafting a will might seem daunting, breaking it down into manageable steps can simplify the process. This guide gives a step-by-step approach to writing your will, highlighting key considerations along the way.

Step 1: Reflect on Your Estate Planning Goals

Before drafting your will, take some time to consider what you aim to achieve. Do you want to ensure that your children are cared for? Are there specific items of sentimental or monetary value you want to leave to certain individuals? Understanding your estate planning goals will guide the decisions you make throughout the will-writing process.

Step 2: Inventory Your Assets

Compile a comprehensive list of your assets, including real estate, bank accounts, investments, insurance policies, personal property, and any digital assets. Estimating the value of these assets will give you a clearer picture of your estate's worth and help you decide how to distribute them.

Step 3: Decide on Beneficiaries

Identify who you want to inherit your assets. Beneficiaries can include family members, friends, charitable organizations, or anyone else you choose. Be as specific as possible in your designations to avoid any ambiguity.

Step 4: Choose an Executor

Select a trusted individual to serve as the executor of your will. This person will be responsible for carrying out the terms of your will, so choose someone who is organized, trustworthy, and capable of handling the responsibilities.

Step 5: Appoint a Guardian for Minor Children

If you have minor children, naming a guardian is one of the most critical decisions in your will. Consider who you would trust to raise your children in your absence, taking into account the potential guardian's values, parenting style, and relationship with your children.

Step 6: Outline the Distribution of Your Assets

Using the inventory you compiled in Step 2, specify how you want your assets to be distributed. You can make general bequests (e.g., dividing your estate among your children) or specific bequests (e.g., leaving a particular piece of jewelry to a friend).

Step 7: Consider Special Provisions

Think about any special provisions you want to include, such as conditions for inheritance, trusts for minor children, or instructions for the care of pets. These provisions can ensure that your assets are used in ways that align with your values and intentions.

Step 8: Draft Your Will

You can draft your will using a lawyer, online legal services, or will-writing software. While DIY options can be cost-effective, consulting with an estate planning attorney can offer you personalized advice and ensure that your will complies with state laws.

Step 9: Sign Your Will in the Presence of Witnesses

For your will to be legally valid, you must sign it in the presence of at least two witnesses, who must also sign the document. The requirements for witnesses vary by jurisdiction, so be sure to adhere to local laws.

Step 10: Store Your Will Safely

Once your will is signed and witnessed, store it in a safe, accessible place. Inform your executor and a trusted family member or friend of its location so that it can be easily found when needed.

Step 11: Review and Update Your Will as Needed

Life changes, such as marriage, divorce, the birth of children, or significant shifts in your assets, can necessitate updates to your will. Periodically review your will and make any necessary amendments to ensure that it continues to reflect your wishes.

Given the importance of crafting a legally sound and clear will, let's explore a practical example to illustrate how one might be structured. Please note, this example is simplified and designed for illustrative purposes only. It's crucial to consult with a legal professional when creating your own will to ensure it meets all legal requirements and accurately reflects your wishes.

Example of a Simple Will

[Introduction]

I, [Your Full Name], residing at [Your Full Address], being of sound mind and not acting under duress or undue influence, hereby declare this document to be my Last Will and Testament, revoking all previously made wills and codicils.

[Appointment of Executor]

I appoint [Executor's Full Name], residing at [Executor's Address], as the Executor of my will. If [Executor's Full Name] is unable or unwilling to serve, I appoint [Alternate Executor's Name] as the alternate Executor.

[Guardianship for Minor Children]

Should I die leaving minor children, I appoint [Guardian's Name], residing at [Guardian's Address], as their guardian to care for their health, education, and welfare. If [Guardian's Name] is unable to serve, I appoint [Alternate Guardian's Name] as the alternate guardian.

[Asset Distribution]

I hereby bequeath my assets as follows:

1. To [Beneficiary #1 Name], I bequeath [specific asset or percentage of estate], free of all taxes and expenses.
2. To [Beneficiary #2 Name], I bequeath [specific asset or percentage of estate], free of all taxes and expenses.
3. Should any of my above-named beneficiaries predecease me, their share of my estate shall be distributed in equal parts to their surviving children, if any.

[Residuary Estate]

All the rest, residue, and remainder of my estate, of whatever kind and wherever located, not effectively disposed of by this will, I give, devise, and bequeath to [Residuary Beneficiary's Name], free of all taxes and expenses.

[Signatures]

IN WITNESS WHEREOF, I have hereunto set my hand this [day] day of [month], [year].

[Your Signature]

[Your Printed Name]

[Witness Acknowledgment]

Signed, declared, and published by [Your Full Name] as and for [his/her] Last Will and Testament, in the presence of us, who, at [his/her] request, in [his/her] presence and in the presence of each other, have subscribed our names as witnesses thereto.

- Witness #1: [Printed Name] [Signature] [Address]
- Witness #2: [Printed Name] [Signature] [Address]

This example demonstrates the basic structure of a simple will, including key sections like the introduction, appointment of an executor and guardian, asset distribution, and signatures. Remember, the specific language and legal requirements for wills vary by jurisdiction, and certain assets might be better managed through other estate planning tools like trusts. Always seek legal advice to ensure your estate plan best suits your needs and complies with local laws.

Testacy, Intestacy and Partial Intestacy

Navigating the concepts of testacy and intestacy is fundamental to understanding estate planning and the importance of having a will. These terms describe whether or not a person has left a valid will at the time of their death and dictate how their estate will be managed and distributed. Here's a detailed look at testacy, intestacy, and the implications of each.

Testacy

Testacy refers to the condition of dying with a valid will in place. A person who dies testate has taken proactive steps to outline how their assets should be distributed among heirs and may have also made arrangements regarding the care of minor children, charitable donations, and other personal desires. The existence of a valid will simplifies the process of estate administration, as it provides clear instructions to be followed by the estate's executor.

Intestacy

Intestacy occurs when a person dies without a valid will. In the absence of a will, state laws, known as intestacy statutes, determine how the deceased's assets will be divided. These laws vary by jurisdiction but generally prioritize spouses, children, and other close relatives as heirs. While intestacy laws aim to distribute assets in a fair and orderly manner, they may not reflect the decedent's personal wishes or unique family dynamics.

Partial Intestacy

In addition to the clear-cut scenarios of testacy (dying with a valid will) and intestacy (dying without a will), there exists a third, often overlooked situation known as partial intestacy. Partial intestacy occurs when a person dies with a will that only covers part of their estate, leaving other assets without specific directions for their distribution. This situation can arise from various circumstances and has its own set of implications.

Understanding Partial Intestacy

Partial intestacy may occur in several situations, including:

- **Omissions**: The decedent's will might not account for all assets, either because they were acquired after the will was drafted and not updated, or simply overlooked.
- **Invalid Provisions**: Parts of the will may be declared invalid by a court due to failing to meet certain legal standards, lack of proper witnesses, or the will not being updated to reflect changes in family structure, like births or divorces.
- **Contested Bequests**: Specific bequests might be successfully contested in court, potentially invalidating that portion of the will.

Implications of Partial Intestacy

When partial intestacy occurs, the distribution of assets not covered by the will falls under the state's intestacy laws. This means that:

- **Mixed Distribution Methods**: While assets mentioned in the will are distributed according to its directives, the remainder that falls under partial intestacy is allocated based on statutory formulas, potentially leading to unintended beneficiaries.
- **Potential for Increased Conflict**: The existence of a will implies specific wishes for asset distribution. However, when assets are left out, it may cause disputes among heirs over who the decedent intended to inherit the unmentioned assets.
- **Increased Legal and Administrative Complexity**: Managing an estate under partial intestacy can complicate the executor's or administrator's duties, potentially leading to longer probate processes and increased costs.

Preventing Partial Intestacy

To avoid the complications associated with partial intestacy, consider the following strategies:

- **Comprehensive Asset Review**: Regularly review and update your will to ensure it accounts for all assets. This includes items acquired after the initial drafting of the will.
- **Residuary Clause**: Including a residuary clause in your will can ensure that any assets not specifically mentioned are still distributed according to your general wishes. This clause covers the "rest, residue, and remainder" of your estate.

- **Legal Consultation**: Regular consultations with an estate planning attorney can help identify potential gaps in your will and ensure that it remains valid and comprehensive in light of changing laws and personal circumstances.

Partial intestacy highlights the necessity of thorough estate planning and regular updates to one's will. While having a will is significantly better than having none at all, ensuring that the will is comprehensive and up-to-date is crucial for fully realizing your estate planning goals. By taking proactive steps to avoid partial intestacy, you can provide clarity, reduce the potential for disputes among your heirs, and ensure that your estate is distributed entirely according to your wishes.

Alternatives to a Will in Estate Planning

While a will is a cornerstone of traditional estate planning, providing clear directives for the distribution of assets upon death, it's not the only tool available for managing your estate. Various instruments can complement or, in some cases, serve as substitutes for a will, each offering unique advantages and considerations. This chapter explores these alternatives, helping you navigate the broader landscape of estate planning.

Living Trusts

A living trust, particularly a revocable living trust, stands out as a popular alternative to a will. Created during your lifetime, it allows you to control your assets within the trust, with the flexibility to modify or revoke the trust as your circumstances change.

Unlike a will, a living trust bypasses the probate process, allowing for a more private and expedited transfer of assets to beneficiaries. Trusts also offer more control over the distribution of assets, enabling you to set conditions or staggered distributions over time.

Establishing and managing a living trust can be more complex and costly than drafting a will, often requiring assistance from an estate planning attorney.

Joint Ownership

Holding property jointly, with rights of survivorship, means that upon the death of one owner, the surviving owner(s) automatically inherit the deceased's share of the property without it passing through probate.

This method provides a straightforward means of asset transfer, particularly useful for spouses or partners wanting to ensure that significant assets like homes and bank accounts remain with the surviving party.

Joint ownership can be complicated by divorce, debt issues, or disagreements between co-owners, and it may not be suitable for all types of property.

Beneficiary Designations

Many financial accounts and insurance policies allow for direct beneficiary designations, meaning the assets or benefits bypass probate and go directly to the named beneficiaries upon the account holder's death.

Designations are easy to set up and change, offering a simple way to ensure that specific assets are transferred quickly to your chosen beneficiaries.

It's crucial to regularly review and update beneficiary designations to reflect changes in your life circumstances and estate planning goals.

Payable-On-Death (POD) and Transfer-On-Death (TOD) Accounts

Similar to beneficiary designations, POD and TOD accounts allow for the direct transfer of assets like bank savings, securities, and even real estate in some jurisdictions, to a named beneficiary upon death.

These designations avoid probate and can be an efficient way to pass on certain types of assets directly to beneficiaries.

As with beneficiary designations, keeping POD and TOD designations current with your estate planning objectives is essential.

Gifts

Gifting assets during your lifetime can be an effective way to reduce your taxable estate and directly benefit your loved ones or charitable organizations ahead of your passing.

Lifetime gifts can bring immediate joy to both giver and receiver and potentially reduce estate taxes.

There are annual and lifetime limits for tax-free gifts, beyond which tax implications may arise. Additionally, gifting can impact your financial security if not carefully planned.

While a will is a foundational element of estate planning, these alternatives can offer additional flexibility, privacy, and efficiency in managing and distributing your assets. In many cases, a combination of these tools, tailored to your unique needs and circumstances, will offer the most comprehensive estate planning solution. Consulting with an estate planning professional is crucial to understanding how these alternatives can work in concert with a will to fulfill your estate planning goals, ensuring that your legacy is preserved and your loved ones are cared for according to your wishes.

Living Trusts

A living trust is an essential component of comprehensive estate planning, offering flexibility, privacy, and control over the management and distribution of your assets both during your lifetime and after your passing. Unlike a will, which comes into effect only after death, a living trust becomes operational the moment it's created and funded, providing immediate benefits. This chapter delves into the mechanics, advantages, and considerations of incorporating a living trust into your estate plan.

Understanding Living Trusts

It is a legal document that places your assets under the management of a trustee for the benefit of your chosen beneficiaries. The person who creates the trust (the grantor) can also serve as the trustee, managing the trust assets during their lifetime. Living trusts are typically revocable, meaning they can be altered or dissolved by the grantor at any time, providing significant flexibility.

Key Components of a Living Trust

A living trust is a dynamic estate planning tool, designed to provide control, protection, and efficiency in managing one's assets. Central to its function are four critical roles: the Grantor, Trustee, Successor Trustee, and Beneficiaries. Each plays a crucial part in the trust's creation, administration, and eventual distribution of assets. Understanding these components in depth is crucial for anyone considering a living trust as part of their estate plan.

Grantor

The Grantor, also known as the Settlor or Trustor, is the individual who creates the trust. The grantor transfers ownership of their assets into the trust, effectively relinquishing personal ownership to be held by the trust itself.

- **Role and Responsibilities**: The grantor decides the trust's terms, including how assets should be managed and distributed. This involves selecting the trustee(s), naming beneficiaries, and outlining any specific conditions or instructions for asset management and distribution.
- **Rights**: In the case of a revocable living trust, the grantor retains the right to modify or revoke the trust entirely during their lifetime. This flexibility allows the grantor to adapt the trust to changing circumstances or wishes.

Trustee

The Trustee is the person or institution appointed by the grantor to manage the trust's assets. This role involves a fiduciary duty, requiring the trustee to act in the best interest of the beneficiaries.

- **Role and Responsibilities**: They are responsible for managing the trust assets according to the terms set out in the trust document. This can include investment decisions, asset distribution, and general administration tasks to ensure the trust's objectives are met.

- **Powers**: Trustees have broad powers, defined by the trust document and state law, to manage, invest, and distribute trust assets. They must, however, always act within the scope of their fiduciary duties and the trust's terms.

Successor Trustee

A Successor Trustee is designated to take over trust management if the original trustee is unable or unwilling to continue, whether due to resignation, incapacity, or death.

- **Role and Transition**: The transition to a successor trustee should be seamless, with the successor immediately assuming all duties and responsibilities of the trustee to ensure continuous management of the trust. This role is critical for maintaining the trust's integrity and fulfilling its purposes, especially in managing assets for beneficiaries who are minors or have special needs.

- **Selection Considerations**: Choosing a successor trustee involves careful consideration of the individual's or institution's ability to manage complex financial matters and adhere to the trust's terms. It's often advisable to discuss the responsibilities with potential successors to ensure they're willing and able to serve.

Beneficiaries

- **Definition**: Beneficiaries are the individuals or entities designated by the grantor to benefit from the trust's assets. They are the ultimate recipients of the trust's income or principal, according to the terms specified by the grantor.

- **Rights and Interests**: Beneficiaries have a vested interest in the trust, with rights defined by the trust document and state law. These can include the right to receive distributions, obtain information about the trust assets and management, and, in some cases, challenge the trustee's decisions if they believe the trustee is not acting in their best interest.

- **Types of Beneficiaries**: A trust can name multiple beneficiaries, including primary and contingent beneficiaries. Primary beneficiaries are the first in line to receive the trust assets, while contingent beneficiaries are next should the primary beneficiaries predecease the grantor or be otherwise unable to inherit.

The well-defined roles of the grantor, trustee, successor trustee, and beneficiaries form the backbone of a living trust, each contributing to the trust's effective operation and the achievement of the grantor's estate planning goals.

Advantages of a Living Trust

Probate Avoidance

The capacity of a living trust to circumvent the probate process is among its most lauded benefits Assets held within a living trust can be transferred directly to beneficiaries upon the grantor's death, sidestepping the often protracted and public probate procedure required for wills. This direct transfer mechanism not only expedites the distribution of assets but also preserves the privacy of the estate and its beneficiaries, a contrast to the probate process which renders estate matters public. Furthermore, avoiding probate translates to significant cost savings, reducing or eliminating the legal and court fees that would otherwise diminish the estate's value, thereby ensuring that beneficiaries receive a larger share of their intended inheritance.

Management During Incapacity

Another critical advantage of a living trust is its provision for the seamless management of the grantor's assets in the event of incapacitation. Should the grantor become unable to manage their affairs due to health reasons, the trust is structured to facilitate an uninterrupted transition of management to a successor trustee. This feature guarantees that the grantor's care and financial responsibilities continue to be met without the need for court intervention, preserving the grantor's autonomy over their estate even in times of vulnerability.

Control Over Asset Distribution

Living trusts afford grantors an unparalleled level of control over the distribution of their assets. Grantors can dictate specific terms under which beneficiaries can access their inheritance, such as age restrictions or conditions related to education and healthcare. This detailed control extends to protections against beneficiaries' potential financial missteps or vulnerabilities, safeguarding the inheritance from creditors or legal claims in the event of a beneficiary's divorce, thereby ensuring that the assets serve the grantor's intended purpose for their beneficiaries.

Privacy

The privacy conferred by a living trust is a significant advantage for many grantors. Unlike wills, which become public documents once they enter the probate process, the contents and provisions of a living trust remain confidential, known only to those directly involved. This level of discretion is particularly valued by those who want to keep the financial details of their estate and the specifics of their beneficiaries' inheritances shielded from public view.

Continuity and Long-Term Planning

For those focused on legacy and long-term planning, living trusts offer a mechanism to ensure continuity beyond the grantor's lifetime. Through the designation of successor trustees, grantors can establish a clear succession plan for their estate, avoiding potential disruptions and maintaining consistent management and distribution of assets according to the grantor's wishes. Moreover, living trusts can be crafted to support charitable endeavors, scholarships, or family foundations for generations, embodying the grantor's values and philanthropic goals far into the future.

The benefits of incorporating a living trust into an estate plan are manifold, encompassing probate avoidance, seamless asset management, granular control over asset distribution, enhanced privacy, and enduring legacy planning. These advantages collectively underscore the living trust's role as a versatile and effective estate planning tool. Engaging with a seasoned estate planning attorney to navigate the intricacies of living trusts can ensure that your estate planning strategy is comprehensively aligned with your long-term goals and the welfare of your beneficiaries.

Establishing a Living Trust

Establishing a living trust is a strategic step in estate planning that, as we saw earlier, provides numerous benefits, including avoiding probate, maintaining privacy, and ensuring assets are managed and distributed according to your wishes. The process involves several detailed steps, each critical for the trust to effectively serve its intended purpose. Here's a in-depth look at how to establish a living trust.

Understanding the Purpose and Types of Trusts

In the realm of estate planning, trusts are versatile instruments designed to manage assets and provide for beneficiaries according to specific terms. Before incorporating a trust into your estate plan, it's crucial to grasp the various types available, each tailored to meet different needs and objectives. This chapter delves into the common types of trusts, helping you navigate the options and select the most appropriate for your situation.

Revocable Living Trust

A **revocable living trust** is created during the grantor's lifetime and can be altered or revoked at any time. The grantor typically serves as the trustee, managing the assets within the trust until death or incapacitation, at which point a designated successor trustee takes over.

- **Purpose**: This type is primarily used to avoid probate, maintain privacy, and manage assets during the grantor's lifetime and after death.
- **Flexibility**: Its revocable nature allows the grantor to retain control over the trust assets and make adjustments as circumstances change.

Irrevocable Trust

Once established, an **irrevocable trust** cannot be easily changed or revoked. The grantor transfers assets into the trust, effectively removing them from personal ownership.

- **Purpose**: This type is often used for asset protection from creditors, reducing estate taxes, and providing for beneficiaries in a way that the assets cannot be claimed by creditors or in divorce settlements.

- **Tax Benefits**: Assets in an irrevocable trust are often exempt from estate taxes, as they are no longer considered part of the grantor's personal estate.

Testamentary Trust

A **testamentary trust** is established through a will and comes into effect upon the grantor's death. Unlike living trusts, it does not avoid probate but can provide for minor children or beneficiaries with specific needs.

- **Purpose**: This type allows for the controlled distribution of assets, according to the terms set forth in the will, after the grantor's death.
- **Controlled Distribution**: Ideal for grantors who want to place conditions on inheritance, such as age-related milestones or specific purposes like education.

Charitable Trust

Charitable trusts are established to benefit a charitable organization or cause. There are two main types: **charitable lead trusts** and **charitable remainder trusts**.

- **Purpose**: This type allow grantors to support charitable causes while potentially providing tax benefits and maintaining some level of income for themselves or other beneficiaries.
- **Tax Advantages**: Contributions to charitable trusts can reduce the taxable estate and offer income tax deductions.

Special Needs Trust

A **special needs trust** is designed to provide for a beneficiary with disabilities without disqualifying them from receiving government assistance, such as Medicaid or Supplemental Security Income.

- **Purpose**: To ensure a beneficiary with special needs can receive inheritance or gifts without affecting their eligibility for public benefits.
- **Controlled Use of Funds**: The trust specifies that funds are to be used for the beneficiary's supplemental needs beyond what government benefits provide.

Spendthrift Trust

A **spendthrift trust** protects the beneficiary's inheritance from creditors and the beneficiary's own potentially imprudent spending.

- **Purpose**: Designed for beneficiaries who may not manage a large sum of money wisely or who have significant debts.
- **Protection**: The trust restricts the beneficiary's direct access to the assets, with distributions controlled by the trustee according to the grantor's instructions.

Selecting the right type of trust for your estate plan depends on your individual goals, whether it's avoiding probate, reducing tax liabilities, protecting assets, or providing for a loved one with special needs. Each type of trust offers unique advantages and limitations. Understanding these options allows you to make informed decisions tailored to your estate planning objectives. Collaborating with an estate planning attorney can further elucidate the nuances of each trust type, ensuring your estate is structured to best serve your and your beneficiaries' interests.

Step To Establish A Trust:

Choosing Between Individual and Joint Trusts

Decide whether you need an individual or join trust, often used by married couples. This decision impacts how assets are managed during your lifetime and distributed upon death, and it may have significant tax implications.

Selecting Your Trustee and Successor Trustee

Choosing a reliable trustee and a successor one is paramount. Initially, you might serve as the trustee of your own trust, managing the assets according to the trust's terms. However, appointing a trustworthy successor trustee ensures that your assets continue to be managed according to your wishes if you become incapacitated or pass away.

Designating Your Beneficiaries

Clearly designate who your beneficiaries will be and what assets they will receive. A living trust allows for specific stipulations regarding how and when beneficiaries access their inheritance, offering you nuanced control over asset distribution.

Drafting the Trust Document

The trust document is the legal instrument that outlines how the trust will operate. It includes your intentions for asset distribution, names the trustee and successor trustee, and identifies the beneficiaries. Given the legal complexities involved, it's advisable to work with an experienced estate planning attorney to draft this document, ensuring it accurately reflects your wishes and complies with state laws.

Funding the Trust

For the trust to take effect, you must transfer ownership of the designated assets into the trust. This process, known as funding the trust, may involve changing titles and deeds to reflect the trust as the new owner of the assets. Proper funding is crucial for the trust to function as intended, and it's a step that should be completed with meticulous attention to detail.

Maintaining and Reviewing the Trust

Once established, the trust should be reviewed and possibly updated periodically to reflect changes in your life circumstances, financial situation, or estate planning goals. Regular maintenance ensures that the trust continues to align with your wishes and the needs of your beneficiaries.

Establishing a living trust involves careful consideration, detailed planning, and strategic decision-making. By thoroughly understanding the process and working with professional advisors, you can create a living trust that provides for efficient management and distribution of your assets, aligns with your estate planning objectives, and secures your legacy for future generations.

Also, when exploring the establishment and use of a living trust it's essential to weigh not only its advantages but also its considerations and limitations. These factors play a critical role in determining whether a living trust is the most appropriate tool for your estate planning needs.

Considerations

Initial Costs and Complexity

The process of setting up a living trust involves more than just drafting and signing a document. It requires a detailed inventory of your assets, decisions on trustees and beneficiaries, and, most importantly, the actual transfer of assets into the trust (funding). These steps can necessitate legal advice and assistance, leading to higher initial costs compared to drafting a simple will. Moreover, the complexity of managing the trust—keeping records, managing assets within the trust, and understanding the legal obligations of a trustee—can be daunting for some.

Maintenance

A living trust is not a set-it-and-forget-it arrangement. As your life circumstances and assets change, so too should your trust. This means that every time you acquire a new significant asset, you must remember to title it in the name of the trust. Failure to do so may leave those assets outside the trust, subject to probate. Regular reviews and updates to the trust document are necessary to reflect changes in your wishes, family structure, or financial situation.

Limitations

Not a Complete Substitute for a Will

While a living trust can manage and distribute most of your assets, there are certain things it cannot do. For instance, only a will can name guardians for minor children. Therefore, even with a living trust, having a will—often a "pour-over" will that directs any assets outside the trust into it upon your death—is advisable. This ensures that all your assets are eventually distributed according to the trust's terms, even those accidentally left out of the from it.

Funding the Trust

One of the most critical steps in creating a living trust is funding it—transferring assets into it. This step is often underestimated and can be an administrative burden. Real estate deeds must be re-titled, bank accounts transferred, and investment accounts re-registered in the name of the trust. Failure to properly fund it can result in assets being left outside the trust, defeating the purpose of avoiding probate.

Legal and Tax Implications

While living trusts offer privacy and avoid probate, they do not inherently offer tax advantages. For most people, a revocable living trust has no effect on income taxes during their lifetime, and assets in the trust are still considered part of the estate for estate tax purposes. Understanding the tax implications and ensuring the trust is structured to meet your tax planning goals requires professional advice.

A living trust is a powerful estate planning tool, offering significant benefits in terms of asset management, privacy, and avoiding probate. However, the decision to use a living trust should be made after careful consideration of its initial setup and ongoing maintenance costs, the complexity of managing the trust, and its limitations compared to a will. Consulting with an estate planning professional can be helpful, ensuring that your estate plan, whether it includes a living trust or other instruments, aligns with your overall objectives and provides for your loved ones as intended.

Things to Look for Before Hiring a Trust Attorney

Selecting the right trust attorney is a pivotal decision in the estate planning process. A trust attorney not only helps in drafting and finalizing your trust documents but also plays a critical role in ensuring that your estate is managed and distributed according to your wishes. Let's see some essential factors to consider and questions to ask before hiring a an attorney, ensuring you choose a professional who aligns with your estate planning objectives.

1. Specialization and Experience

Look for an attorney whose primary area of practice is estate planning. This specialization ensures they are well-versed in the nuances of trust law and stay updated on any changes.

Inquire about the attorney's experience, specifically how long they have been practicing in the field of estate planning. Experience often correlates with the ability to handle complex situations and can give sound advice.

2. Trust Administration Services

Confirm whether the attorney offers trust administration services. An attorney prepared to administer the trust they create for you demonstrates confidence in their work and delivers continuity for your family members in executing your estate plan.

3. Certification and Qualifications

Check if the attorney is a certified specialist in estate planning. This certification is a testament to their expertise, experience, and commitment to their practice area. It often involves passing additional exams and meeting specific practice requirements.

4. Comprehensive Practice Focus

Ensure the attorney focuses exclusively or primarily on estate planning and related areas. Attorneys practicing in multiple unrelated areas may not have the depth of knowledge needed for effective estate planning.

5. Client Engagement and Communication

Favor attorneys who offer initial consultations. This meeting is an opportunity to gauge their communication style, understanding of your needs, and how they plan to address your estate planning goals.

The right attorney should be able to explain complex legal concepts in understandable terms. Clarity in communication is crucial for ensuring you are fully informed about your estate planning choices.

6. Client Testimonials and Reviews

Look for testimonials and reviews from previous clients. Positive feedback can give insight into the attorney's working style, reliability, and effectiveness in handling estate planning matters.

7. Fees and Billing

Discuss the attorney's fees upfront. Whether they charge a flat fee for estate planning services or bill hourly, understanding the cost structure is important to avoid surprises.

Questions to Ask:

1. **How do you stay current with estate planning laws and practices?**
2. **Can you provide examples of how you've handled complex estate planning scenarios?**
3. **What is your approach to estate planning for families with unique circumstances, such as blended families or special needs trusts?**
4. **How do you ensure that the trust reflects my specific wishes and goals?**
5. **What support can my family expect in administering the trust after my passing?**

Choosing the right trust attorney is more than a matter of expertise; it's about finding a professional who understands your vision for the future and can guide you through the estate planning process with compassion and competence. By asking the right questions and evaluating potential attorneys based on their specialization, experience, communication, and commitment to your needs, you can establish a trust that effectively safeguards your legacy and provides for your loved ones according to your wishes.

What to Do When the Trust Owner/Grantor Dies

The death of a trust owner, also known as the grantor, marks a significant transition point in the lifecycle of a trust. This chapter outlines the essential steps and considerations for trustees and beneficiaries to navigate this period effectively, ensuring that the grantor's wishes are honored and the trust's assets are managed and distributed according to the established terms.

Immediate Actions and Notifications

1. **Obtain Death Certificates**: Secure multiple certified copies of the death certificate. These are required for various administrative and legal purposes, including notifying financial institutions and transferring assets.

2. **Notify Relevant Parties**: Inform all beneficiaries of the trust, as well as any institutions holding trust assets (banks, brokerage firms, etc.), about the grantor's death.

3. **Review the Trust Document**: Carefully read the agreement to understand its terms, the distribution plan, and your responsibilities as the trustee.

4. **Legal and Financial Consultation**: Consider consulting with an estate planning attorney and a financial advisor who specialize in trusts to guide you through the process and ensure compliance with state laws and tax regulations.

Transitioning the Trust

1. **Transition to Irrevocable Trust**: Upon the grantor's death, a revocable trust typically becomes irrevocable, meaning no further changes can be made to its terms. The trustee must now manage the trust according to its established directives.

2. **Apply for an Employer Identification Number (EIN)**: Since the trust now operates as a separate legal entity, apply for an EIN from the IRS. This number is used for tax filings and managing trust assets.

Asset Management

1. **Inventory of Assets**: Create a comprehensive inventory of all assets held within the trust, including real estate, bank accounts, investments, and personal property.

2. **Valuation of Assets**: Determine the fair market value of trust assets as of the date of the grantor's death. This valuation is crucial for tax purposes and equitable asset distribution.

3. **Management and Distribution of Assets**: Follow the trust's directives for asset distribution. This may involve selling assets, distributing them directly to beneficiaries, or continuing to manage them on behalf of the beneficiaries.

Tax Implications

1. **Filing Trust Taxes**: File IRS Form 1041, the U.S. Income Tax Return for Estates and Trusts, to report any income the trust earns after the grantor's death.
2. **Final Personal Tax Returns**: Prepare and file the grantor's final personal tax return (IRS Form 1040), reporting any income earned up to the date of death.
3. **Consider Distribution Strategies**: To minimize the trust's tax burden, consider distributing income to beneficiaries, who may be subject to lower tax rates.

Ongoing Trust Administration

1. **Maintain Records**: Keep detailed records of all transactions, communications, and decisions related to the trust's administration.
2. **Annual Reviews**: Conduct annual reviews of the trust's performance and compliance with its terms, adjusting strategies as needed to fulfill your fiduciary duties effectively.
3. **Communicate with Beneficiaries**: Maintain open and transparent communication with beneficiaries regarding the trust's administration and any distributions or decisions made.

The death of a trust grantor initiates a series of critical steps for trustees to ensure the trust is administered according to its terms and legal requirements. By carefully managing assets, understanding tax obligations, and fulfilling fiduciary duties with diligence and integrity, trustees can honor the grantor's legacy and safeguard the interests of the beneficiaries. Always consider seeking professional advice to navigate the complexities of trust administration and ensure compliance with all legal and financial obligations.

Inventorying Your Assets

The first practical step in establishing a living trust is to take a comprehensive inventory of your assets. This includes identifying all tangible and intangible assets you own, such as real estate, vehicles, bank accounts, investments, and personal property of value. This inventory will help determine which assets you want to include in the trust and ensure that nothing is overlooked in the estate planning process.

Assets Best Placed in a Trust

When planning your estate, deciding which assets to place in a trust can significantly impact the efficiency, privacy, and control over how your estate is managed and distributed upon your death or incapacitation. Here's a closer look at the types of assets that are typically best suited for inclusion in a trust, given their potential for simplifying the probate process, providing for beneficiaries, and ensuring a seamless transition of assets.

Real Estate

- **Primary Residence and Other Properties**: Real estate is often one of the most valuable assets an individual owns. Including your primary residence, vacation homes, rental properties, or any other real estate holdings in a trust can avoid the often lengthy and public probate process, directly transferring ownership to the trust's beneficiaries according to your wishes.

Financial Accounts

- **Bank Accounts**: Checking, savings, and other bank accounts can be placed in a trust, allowing for immediate access by the trustee to pay for final expenses, debts, or distributions to beneficiaries without going through probate.

- **Investment Accounts**: Brokerage accounts, stocks, and bonds held in a trust can continue to be managed effectively without interruption upon the grantor's death, providing both potential growth and income for beneficiaries specified in the trust.

Business Interests

- **Sole Proprietorships, Partnerships, and LLCs**: Including your interests in businesses ensures that there's a clear line of succession and management directives, preventing potential disputes and operational disruptions. It allows for a predetermined transfer of control and ownership that aligns with your business and personal estate planning goals.

Valuable Personal Property

- **Art, Jewelry, Collectibles**: High-value personal items can be subject to disputes among heirs. Placing them in a trust can clarify your intentions for these items, ensuring they go to the intended beneficiary and potentially avoiding family conflict.

Life Insurance Policies

- While life insurance proceeds are generally not subject to probate, owning the policy within an irrevocable trust (like an ILIT, which we'll discuss later in the book) can offer additional benefits, such as removing the proceeds from your taxable estate and more nuanced control over the distribution of proceeds.

Intellectual Property

- **Copyrights, Patents, Trademarks**: Intellectual property rights can generate significant income and thus have substantial value. Including these assets in a trust ensures that any revenue they produce is distributed according to your estate planning wishes and that the rights are managed or transferred in an orderly manner.

Other Considerations for Trust Inclusion

- **Assets with Sentimental Value**: Items that may not have significant monetary value but hold sentimental importance can also be included in a trust to ensure they are passed on as you wish, potentially avoiding disputes that can arise when such preferences are not legally documented.

Digital Assets in Trusts

In an era where digital footprints expand with every click, post, and transaction, understanding how to manage digital assets within trusts is becoming an essential component of comprehensive estate planning.

Understanding Digital Assets

Digital assets encompass a wide array of online accounts and properties, from the tangible—like cryptocurrencies and online banking—to the intangible, such as social media profiles, blogs, and digital copyrights. As these assets can hold significant financial and sentimental value, their careful consideration in estate planning is crucial.

The Importance of Including Digital Assets in Trusts

- **Asset Protection and Privacy**: Including digital assets in trusts safeguards them from unauthorized access and potential cyber threats, ensuring privacy and security.
- **Avoiding Probate**: Like physical assets, digital assets can be ensnared in probate if not properly managed in a trust, leading to potential legal complications and delays in asset distribution.
- **Generational Wealth Transfer**: Digital assets, particularly those generating ongoing income like royalties or revenue from online businesses, can provide long-term financial benefits to beneficiaries.

Categorizing Digital Assets for Trusts

To effectively include digital assets in a trust, categorizing them based on their nature and the goals for each can simplify the management.

1. **Financial Digital Assets**: This includes cryptocurrencies, online bank accounts, and investment portfolios. These require secure management and clear instructions for access and distribution.
2. **Social and Personal Digital Assets**: Social media accounts, emails, and digital photos often hold sentimental value and may need specific instructions for memorialization or deletion.
3. **Intellectual Property and Online Businesses**: Copyrights, digital content, blogs, and e-commerce platforms not only have financial value but also require ongoing management and strategy for revenue generation.

Practical Steps for Including Digital Assets in Trusts

1. **Inventory of Digital Assets**: Compile a comprehensive list of digital assets, including login credentials and instructions for access. This list, however, should be kept secure and separate from the trust document for privacy reasons.

2. **Use of Digital Asset Trusts**: Consider establishing a separate digital asset trust or incorporating digital asset clauses in a broader trust to specify management and distribution wishes.

3. **Selecting a Digital Executor**: Appoint a trustee or executor who is tech-savvy and understands the value and nature of your digital assets. This individual will be responsible for executing your wishes concerning your digital estate.

4. **Legal and Tax Implications**: Consult with estate planning professionals to understand the legal and tax implications of transferring digital assets into a trust, especially for assets that may have significant financial value or potential for appreciation.

5. **Regular Updates**: Digital assets can change rapidly. Regularly updating your trust documents to reflect new assets or changes in digital asset laws is essential for ensuring ongoing relevance and effectiveness.

Strategically selecting assets for inclusion in a trust can significantly enhance the effectiveness of your estate plan. It's not just about the legal and financial advantages; it's also about peace of mind, knowing your assets will be managed and distributed according to your explicit wishes. Always consider consulting with an estate planning attorney to ensure your trust is properly set up and funded, aligning with your overall estate planning goals and providing for your beneficiaries in the best way possibl

Managing Your Digital Legacy

- **The Legal Framework: RUFADAA**

The Revised Uniform Fiduciary Access to Digital Assets Act (RUFADAA) offers a legal structure that enables individuals to direct the future of their digital assets. Adopted by many states, RUFADAA allows you to outline how you want your digital assets to be accessed and distributed after your death. This act ensures your digital footprint can be managed as per your intentions, mirroring the care you'd take with physical assets.

- **Tools Provided by Digital Platforms**

Many digital platforms and services, recognizing the need for posthumous digital asset management, offer built-in tools that allow users to specify future access or the handling of their accounts. Services like Google's Inactive Account Manager and Facebook's Legacy

Contact feature empower you to decide how your digital presence is curated and who can oversee your accounts in your absence.

Incorporating Digital Assets into Estate Documents

For digital assets or platforms that lack bespoke posthumous management tools, or if you've not specified your wishes through these tools, traditional estate planning documents become essential. By including digital asset instructions in your will, trust, or power of attorney, you ensure that all aspects of your digital estate are considered and controlled, from your online financial records to personal photographs and social media accounts.

Navigating Terms of Service Agreements

Digital assets are governed by the terms of service agreements of each platform, which can dictate what happens to your accounts upon your death. While these agreements vary, your proactive planning through platform-specific tools or broader legal documents generally takes precedence, ensuring your digital legacy is handled according to your specific desires.

The Importance of Proactive Digital Estate Planning

Your digital assets are an extension of your personal and financial life, warranting the same attention and care in estate planning as your physical assets. Understanding RUFADAA, utilizing platform-specific management tools, and incorporating digital assets into your estate planning documents are critical steps in safeguarding your digital legacy. By taking action now, you ensure that your digital presence is managed respectfully and in alignment with your wishes, providing clarity and ease for those you leave behind. Engaging with an estate planning professional can further refine this process, tailoring your digital estate plan to your unique circumstances.

Assets to Consider Leaving Out of a Trust

While trusts are versatile tools for estate planning, not all assets benefit from being placed in a trust. In some cases, including certain assets can complicate your estate plan without providing significant advantages. Here's a look at assets you might consider leaving out of a trust:

Retirement Accounts

- **Individual Retirement Accounts (IRAs), 401(k)s, and Other Retirement Plans**: These accounts are designed with specific tax advantages that could be compromised if transferred into a trust. Since these accounts already avoid probate through designated beneficiary forms, placing them in a trust is generally unnecessary and can lead to unfavorable tax consequences.

Health Savings Accounts (HSAs) and Medical Savings Accounts (MSAs)

- **HSAs and MSAs**: Similar to retirement accounts, these health-related savings accounts are tied to individual beneficiaries and offer tax benefits that are best utilized outside of a trust framework. Including them in a trust could inadvertently trigger tax issues or disrupt the intended flow of benefits.

Vehicles Used for Personal Use

- **Cars, Boats, and Other Personal Vehicles**: These assets are typically not ideal for trust inclusion due to the frequency of change in ownership (buying and selling) and the relative ease of transferring ownership upon death through other means. Additionally, transferring a vehicle into a trust might raise insurance complications or liability issues.

Personal Checking Accounts

- **Day-to-Day Checking Accounts**: While savings and investment accounts might benefit from being in a trust, a personal checking account used for daily transactions might not need the same level of oversight and can complicate access to funds needed for regular expenses.

Property with High Debt

- **Mortgaged Real Estate or Other Heavily Leveraged Assets**: Including assets with significant debt in a trust can create unnecessary complexity, particularly if the debt outweighs the asset's value or if managing the debt becomes cumbersome within the trust structure.

Certain Types of Personal Property

- **Low-Value Items and Personal Effects**: Items that do not have significant monetary value and can be easily distributed without formal legal processes might not need to be included in a trust. The administrative burden of cataloging and managing these items in a trust may outweigh the benefits.

Jointly Owned Property

- **Assets Owned with Rights of Survivorship**: Property owned jointly, especially with rights of survivorship (as is common with marital assets), automatically passes to the surviving owner upon death, bypassing probate without the need for trust inclusion.

Deciding which assets to include or exclude from your trust is a nuanced process that requires careful consideration of each asset's characteristics, the tax implications, and how you would like to manage and distribute your estate. While trusts offer significant benefits for estate planning, they are not a one-size-fits-all solution, and some assets may be better managed outside of this framework. Consulting with an estate planning professional can offer clarity and guidance tailored to your unique situation, ensuring your estate plan aligns with your goals and provides for your beneficiaries as efficiently as possible.

Trusts vs. Wills: A Comprehensive Comparison

In navigating the landscape of estate planning, the choice between utilizing a trust or a will—or a combination of both—requires a nuanced understanding of how each tool aligns with your personal and financial goals. While both trusts and wills serve the fundamental purpose of guiding the distribution of your assets after your passing, they operate within different legal and procedural frameworks, each offering unique advantages and considerations.

The decision often hinges on several key factors: the need for probate avoidance, the desire for privacy, the complexity of your estate, and the level of control you want to maintain over asset distribution. Trusts, particularly living trusts, stand out for their ability to bypass the probate process, facilitating a quicker and more private transfer of assets to beneficiaries. This feature not only expedites the distribution process but also shields the details of your estate from becoming public record—a consideration for those prioritizing discretion in their estate planning.

On the other hand, wills, while subject to probate, provide a straightforward and traditionally less expensive route for expressing your final wishes. They are indispensable for appointing guardians for minor children, a critical aspect that trusts cannot address. Wills offer a clear, legally recognized framework for asset distribution and can be especially suitable for estates that may not benefit significantly from the probate avoidance offered by trusts.

Cost and complexity also play pivotal roles in the decision-making process. Trusts typically involve more intricate setup procedures, including the need to actively manage and fund the trust, which can incur higher initial costs. Conversely, the simplicity and lower upfront cost of drafting a will make it an accessible option for many, though potential probate costs and the public nature of the process are important to consider.

Ultimately, the choice between a trust and a will is not mutually exclusive. Many estate plans benefit from incorporating both tools, using a trust for the majority of asset management and distribution, complemented by a will for appointing guardianship for minors and covering assets not placed in the trust. This dual approach harnesses the strengths of each tool, providing a comprehensive strategy for estate management and legacy planning.

In summary, while trusts offer probate avoidance, privacy, and detailed control over asset distribution, wills present a simpler, more straightforward means of expressing final wishes, particularly for less complex estates or when appointing guardians for minors. Balancing these considerations against your personal estate planning objectives will guide you in selecting the most appropriate tools for ensuring your legacy is preserved according to your wishes.

Powers of Attorney

In the voyage of estate planning, setting up a Power of Attorney (POA) is like appointing a trusted captain for your ship, ensuring it continues its journey smoothly, even in your absence. The Power of Attorney, a pivotal legal document, empowers another individual to make decisions on your behalf, covering financial dealings and healthcare directives. Now we'll explore the importance of POAs, guiding you through selecting the right person, and highlights common pitfalls to avoid, incorporating practical wisdom and real-world scenarios.

The Essence of Power of Attorney

A POA becomes crucial when life's uncertainties unfold—be it through sudden illness, incapacity, or prolonged absence. Without a POA, your family might face the daunting prospect of court interventions for guardianship or interdiction, a process that is not only emotionally taxing but also financially draining. A well-considered POA can circumvent these challenges, providing a clear, legal pathway for managing your affairs seamlessly.

Types Of POA

In estate planning, understanding the nuances of Power of Attorney (POA) types is crucial. Each type serves a specific purpose, tailored to different needs and scenarios. Here's an overview of the four primary POA types, shedding light on their distinct roles and applications.

General Power of Attorney

A General Power of Attorney grants broad powers to the agent (also known as the attorney-in-fact), allowing them to manage a wide range of financial and legal matters on behalf of the principal. This type of POA can encompass everything from handling financial transactions and managing real estate affairs to dealing with government benefits. It's a comprehensive tool, effective for general estate management or when the principal will be unavailable or incapacitated for a time. However, its broad scope demands a high level of trust in the agent, as it grants them considerable control over the principal's assets and affairs.

Special or Limited Power of Attorney

Contrastingly, a Special or Limited Power of Attorney narrows the agent's authority to specific duties or a particular time frame. This POA is often used for one-off transactions or situations where the principal cannot be present but needs certain tasks completed, such as selling a property, managing specific investments, or handling tax matters. Its limited nature helps maintain tighter control over the scope of authority granted, making it a precise tool for targeted financial or legal actions.

Durable Power of Attorney

The Durable Power of Attorney stands out for its resilience; it remains in effect even if the principal becomes incapacitated, ensuring continuous management of the principal's affairs without court intervention. This type can be general or limited in scope but is distinguished by its durability under circumstances that would typically revoke a POA, such as the principal's severe illness or disability. It's particularly valuable for long-term planning, addressing the need for someone to manage your affairs if you're unable to make decisions yourself.

Medical or Healthcare Power of Attorney

A Medical or Healthcare Power of Attorney specifically grants the agent the authority to make healthcare decisions on the principal's behalf, should they become unable to do so. This type of POA becomes active under conditions defined by the principal, typically relating to their medical incapacitation. It covers decisions ranging from treatment options and medical care to end-of-life wishes, aligning medical actions with the principal's healthcare preferences and values. It's an essential component of healthcare planning, ensuring that medical decisions are made by someone who understands the principal's wishes and has their best interests at heart.

Choosing Your Power of Attorney: A Decision of Trust

The choice of a POA transcends mere administrative delegation; it's about selecting an individual who will stand in your shoes, wielding the power to affect significant life and financial outcomes based on your incapacitation or absence. This role could encompass managing your finances, making critical healthcare decisions, or both, depending on the type of POA selected. Thus, the decision is as much about emotional intelligence and trustworthiness as it is about competence and financial acumen.

Qualities of an Ideal POA

When considering candidates for your POA, reflect on the following attributes:

- **Trustworthiness**: Above all, the agent must be someone you trust implicitly. This person will have access to sensitive information and control over crucial aspects of your life.
- **Reliability**: The ability to rely on your POA to act in your best interests consistently and to fulfill their duties responsibly is non-negotiable.
- **Financial Literacy**: For a financial POA, choose someone with a sound understanding of financial matters and the acumen to manage your assets prudently.
- **Strong Communication Skills**: Your POA should be able to communicate effectively with family members, financial institutions, and healthcare providers, among others.
- **Alignment with Your Values**: Especially for a healthcare POA, it's vital that the agent understands and respects your healthcare choices and values.

The Process of Selection

1. **Self-Reflection**: Begin with introspection. Consider your values, preferences, and the complexity of the decisions your POA might need to make. This understanding will guide your selection process.

2. **Family Discussions**: Engage in open and honest conversations with family members about your considerations for a POA. These discussions can help alleviating concerns, and ensure that your family understands your choices.

3. **Consider the Dynamics**: Reflect on the dynamics between your chosen POA and other family members. The right POA not only respects your wishes but also navigates family relationships diplomatically.

4. **Seek Advice**: Consult with legal and financial advisors to understand the implications of your POA choice and to ensure that your decision aligns with your overall estate plan.

5. **Communicate with Potential Agents**: Before making your decision, have detailed discussions with potential POAs. Ensure they understand the responsibilities, are willing to take on the role, and respect your wishes.

Making the Choice Official

Once you've chosen your POA, formalizing the decision through proper legal documentation is crucial. This process varies by jurisdiction but generally involves signing the POA document in the presence of witnesses or a notary public. Be sure to review the requirements specific to your location with your attorney.

Also remember that life changes, and so might your choice of POA. Regularly review your POA designation as part of your estate planning check-ups. Life events such as marriage, divorce, the birth of children, or the death of a chosen agent may necessitate a change in your POA.

Selecting a Power of Attorney is a profound testament to trust and a cornerstone of comprehensive estate planning. It demands careful consideration, not just of the agent's qualifications but of their alignment with your values and wishes. By approaching this decision with the seriousness it warrants, engaging in open family dialogues, and ensuring legal formalization, you lay a foundation for your wishes to be respected and your legacy to be protected, even in your absence.

Common Missteps in Designating a Power of Attorney

The designation of a Power of Attorney (POA) is an indispensable element in the fabric of comprehensive estate planning. It serves as a safeguard, ensuring that someone you trust can manage your affairs if you're unable to do so yourself. However, the path to establishing a POA is fraught with potential missteps that can undermine the very protection it's meant to offer. Drawing from the insightful guidance of estate planning experts, this chapter illuminates common pitfalls in designating a POA and how to avoid them.

The Perils of Not Having a POA

The absence of a POA can plunge families into legal turmoil, particularly if one becomes incapacitated without having appointed an agent. Such situations often necessitate going through guardianship or interdiction proceedings, which are not only emotionally taxing but also financially draining. The presence of a POA steers clear of these complications, ensuring that your affairs are managed seamlessly, in line with your desires.

Choosing the Right Agent

The heart of a POA is your chosen agent, who will wield considerable influence over your financial and healthcare decisions. The selection process cannot be overstated; it requires discernment beyond familial ties or emotional connections. An agent's reliability and their commitment to acting in your best interest are paramount. Missteps in this area can lead to financial abuses, such as failure to keep accurate records, self-dealing, misappropriation of funds, or even outright theft. Beware of situations where potential agents might exert undue influence, coercing you into granting them unwarranted financial control.

The Devil in the Details

A vaguely drafted POA is a recipe for ambiguity, potentially leaving your agent powerless when clarity is most needed. Precision in defining the scope of the agent's authority ensures that your POA is both effective and enforceable. Furthermore, failing to appoint a backup or alternate agent overlooks the reality that the unexpected can happen to anyone. An agent may become unable or unwilling to serve; having a secondary agent listed can prevent a vacuum of authority.

Complications also arise when multiple agents are required to act together. While this might seem like a measure of added security, it can hamstring decision-making in critical times. Allowing for joint or separate action offers flexibility and ensures that your affairs continue to be managed without delay.

Legal and Institutional Acknowledgment

Another oversight is not considering the legal and institutional requirements for a POA. Some states have specific stipulations for appointing a guardian or curator in the event of incapacity—designations that can be incorporated into your POA to streamline future legal proceedings. Similarly, financial institutions may have their own forms or prerequisites for recognizing a POA. Engaging with these institutions to understand and comply with their requirements can forestall rejection of your POA document at crucial junctures.

Understanding the POA's Limits

A common misunderstanding is the belief that a POA's authority extends beyond the principal's death. It's vital to recognize that a POA ceases upon the principal's death, at which point the executor of the will or the successor trustee of a trust takes over the management of the estate. This distinction underscores the need for a holistic approach to estate planning, integrating a POA with other estate planning tools to cover all bases.

Crafting a POA is a nuanced process that demands careful thought, clear communication, and an understanding of the legal landscape. By avoiding these common pitfalls—through meticulous selection of your agent, specific detailing of powers, preparation for contingencies, and compliance with legal and institutional norms—you safeguard not only your assets and decisions but also the well-being of those you hold dear.

Estate Planning for Blended Families

Blended families, characterized by spouses with children from previous relationships, present unique challenges and considerations in estate planning. The goal is to ensure a fair and intended distribution of assets while honoring the complex relationships within the family. This chapter explores effective strategies for estate planning in blended families, focusing on achieving balance, fairness, and clarity.

Understanding the Complexity

Blended families may involve various dynamics, including children from past marriages, stepchildren, and possibly joint children of the current marriage. Each of these relationships may carry different expectations and obligations, making estate planning a sensitive task that requires thoughtful navigation.

Key Considerations in Estate Planning

1. **Open Communication**: Start with open discussions among family members about estate planning goals and expectations. This can help in understanding everyone's perspective and minimizing potential conflicts.
2. **Fairness vs. Equality**: Recognize that fair distribution may not always mean equal distribution. Factors such as the age of children, their financial needs, and previous inheritances or gifts may influence how assets are allocated.
3. **Use of Trusts**: Trusts can be particularly useful in estate planning for blended families. They offer flexibility in specifying how, when, and to whom assets are distributed.

- **Separate Trusts for Separate Assets**: Consider setting up separate trusts for children from previous relationships and for the current marriage to clearly define the distribution of specific assets.
- **QTIP Trusts**: A Qualified Terminable Interest Property (QTIP) trust allows you to provide for your surviving spouse during their lifetime, with the remainder of the assets then passing to your children from a previous relationship.
- **Lifetime Trusts for Children**: Creating lifetime trusts for children can protect their inheritance until they reach a mature age, as decided by you, ensuring they are financially responsible enough to manage their inheritance.

Navigating the Legal Landscape

1. **Prenuptial Agreements**: For those entering into a marriage with significant assets or children from previous relationships, a prenuptial agreement can clarify what happens to those assets in the event of death or divorce.
2. **Beneficiary Designations**: Pay close attention to beneficiary designations on retirement accounts, insurance policies, and other assets. These designations often supersede wills and trusts, so they should be updated to reflect your current estate planning wishes.
3. **Guardianship Considerations**: If you have minor children, consider who will be their guardian. This decision is crucial, especially if both biological parents are not present or available to take on the role.

Estate Planning Strategies

1. **Stepchild Inclusion**: Legally, stepchildren do not automatically inherit unless specifically named in a will or trust. If you decide to include them in your estate plan, explicitly state this intention in your estate documents.
2. **Regular Updates**: Estate plans should not be static. Regularly review and update your estate planning documents to reflect changes in family dynamics, financial situations, and individual relationships.
3. **Professional Guidance**: Due to the complexities involved, seek the assistance of an estate planning attorney who has experience with blended family dynamics. They can provide customized advice and ensure that your estate plan meets legal requirements while fulfilling your wishes.

Estate planning for blended families requires facing unique challenges with sensitivity and precision. By employing clear communication, thoughtful strategies, and professional guidance, you can create an estate plan that respects and honors the complexity of your family structure. The aim is to ensure that your legacy is passed on according to your wishes, providing for your loved ones in a manner that is fair, balanced, and reflective of your relationships and values.

PART III: TAX PLANNING STRATEGIES

In estate planning, understanding the intricate web of tax implications is essential. Now we'll venture into the often-daunting world of taxes as they pertain to estate planning, with a focus on elucidating the complex interplay between various tax obligations and strategic estate management. It's essential to grasp that the decisions made today, in the context of estate planning, are deeply intertwined with tax implications that can significantly impact the legacy left for your beneficiaries.

Taxes in estate planning extend beyond mere numerical calculations; they embody a critical element that shapes the structure and efficacy of an estate plan. From federal estate taxes that may consume a portion of your estate's value, to state-level inheritance taxes and the nuances of gift taxes during one's lifetime, each tax type brings its unique considerations. Furthermore, the taxation of specific assets, such as retirement accounts and real estate, introduces additional layers to an already complex planning process. A comprehensive understanding of these tax dimensions is crucial for any individual embarking on estate planning.

The objective of this chapter is not to overwhelm but to inform and guide. Through a detailed examination of tax considerations, I aim to arm you with the knowledge and tools necessary to navigate the tax landscape effectively. This exploration is designed to arm you with strategies to minimize tax liabilities, ensuring the preservation of your estate's value for the benefit of your heirs.

Tax laws and regulations are ever-evolving, making the intersection of taxes and estate planning a dynamic and sometimes unpredictable field. The serious nature of these decisions requires a meticulous approach, underpinned by current legal and tax framework understanding. As we delve deeper into this critical aspect of estate planning, remember that the ultimate goal is to ensure that your legacy is passed on according to your wishes, with minimal tax burden on your beneficiaries.

Understanding Estate Taxes: Definition and Applicability

Definition of Estate Taxes

Estate taxes are calculated on the total value of a deceased person's estate before it is distributed to the heirs. This tax is predicated on the "gross estate" value, which encompasses all assets owned at death: cash and securities, real estate, insurance, trusts, annuities, business interests, and other assets. Key to this definition is understanding that estate taxes are levied on the estate's overall value, not on the individual beneficiaries receiving the assets. The tax applies regardless of whether the assets pass via a will, according to state law (in the case of intestacy), or through a trust.

Federal Estate Taxes

The federal government imposes estate taxes at a rate that varies depending on the estate's value beyond a certain exemption threshold. This threshold is adjusted periodically to reflect changes in policy and inflation. As of recent times, only estates valued above this exemption amount are subject to federal estate taxes, making it a concern primarily for high-net-worth individuals. For estates that do owe tax, the rate is progressive, increasing with the estate's value.

One critical aspect of federal estate taxes is the portability feature for married couples, allowing the surviving spouse to use any unused portion of the deceased spouse's exemption. This effectively doubles the exemption amount available to couples, further reducing the number of estates subject to federal estate tax.

State Estate Taxes

While not all states impose an estate tax, those that do have varying rates and exemption thresholds, often significantly lower than the federal exemption. Some states mirror the federal estate tax system but with lower exemption amounts, meaning that an estate could owe state estate tax even if it owes no federal estate tax. State estate taxes require careful planning, particularly for residents or property owners in those states, to minimize potential tax liabilities.

It's important for estate planners and individuals to understand the specific rules and rates applicable in their state or any state where they own property. This understanding is crucial for creating an estate plan that accurately accounts for potential state estate tax liabilities.

Applicability of Estate Taxes

The applicability of estate taxes hinges on several factors:

- **Total Value of the Estate**: Only estates valued above the applicable federal or state exemption thresholds are subject to estate taxes. Determining this value involves a comprehensive appraisal of all assets at the time of death.
- **Marital Deduction**: Assets passed to a surviving spouse are generally exempt from estate taxes at the federal level, thanks to the unlimited marital deduction. This exemption is a cornerstone in planning for married couples, allowing for strategic asset transfer with minimized tax impact.

- **Charitable Deduction**: Assets left to qualified charitable organizations are deductible from the gross estate, potentially reducing the estate's taxable value.

Estate taxes represent a significant aspect of estate planning for individuals with substantial assets. Understanding the nuances of these taxes—how they're defined, calculated, and applied—enables more effective estate planning. Strategic decisions, such as gifting during one's lifetime, establishing trusts, or making charitable donations, can significantly reduce the estate's tax burden, ensuring that more of one's legacy is preserved for future generations.

Federal Estate Tax Thresholds and Rates

Federal estate tax represents a pivotal consideration for individuals seeking to safeguard their financial legacy. The thresholds and rates associated with this tax have undergone significant changes over the years, reflecting shifts in policy and economic conditions. The next pages will dive into the intricacies of federal estate tax thresholds and rates as of 2024, offering a comprehensive guide to navigating these regulations effectively.

The 2024 Federal Estate Tax Exemption

As of 2024, the federal estate tax exemption threshold has been set at $13.61 million for individuals, marking a continuation of the trend towards higher exemption levels. This increase means that estates valued below this amount are exempt from federal estate taxes, a provision that extends significant relief to a vast majority of estates. For married couples, the exemption effectively doubles, allowing estates valued at up to $27.22 million to bypass federal estate taxation, underscoring the importance of strategic estate planning in maximizing this benefit.

Historical Context and Its Impact on Planning

The journey to the current exemption threshold has been marked by significant milestones. Notably, in 2011, the combined exemption for estates and lifetime gifts was set at $5 million, adjusted for inflation. This baseline was made permanent in 2013, reflecting a commitment to shielding more estates from the reach of federal estate taxes. The trajectory from a $5.49 million exemption for individuals in 2017 to the current threshold illustrates the dynamic nature of estate tax law, highlighting the need for continuous monitoring and adaptation in estate planning strategies.

Navigating Federal Estate Tax Rates

For estates that exceed the 2024 exemption threshold of $13.61 million, understanding the applicable tax rates is crucial. The federal estate tax employs a progressive rate structure, where the tax rate increases with the value of the estate beyond the exemption amount. Rates start at 18% for the initial taxable amount and can escalate up to 40% for amounts exceeding $1 million over the threshold. This progressive system necessitates careful planning to minimize tax liabilities, especially for estates hovering near or above the exemption limit.

Taxable Amount	Estate Tax Rate	What You Pay
$1 – $10,000	18%	$0 base tax + 18% on taxable amount
$10,000 – $20,000	20%	$1,800 base tax + 20% on taxable amount
$20,000 – $40,000	22%	$3,800 base tax + 22% on taxable amount
$40,000 – $60,000	24%	$8,200 base tax + 24% on taxable amount
$60,000 – $80,000	26%	$13,000 base tax + 26% on taxable amount
$80,000 – $100,000	28%	$18,200 base tax + 28% on taxable amount
$100,000 – $150,000	30%	$23,800 base tax + 30% on taxable amount
$150,000 – $250,000	32%	$38,800 base tax + 32% on taxable amount
$250,001 – $500,000	34%	$70,800 base tax + 34% on taxable amount
$500,001 – $750,000	37%	$155,800 base tax + 37% on taxable amount
$750,001 – $1 million	39%	$248,300 base tax + 39% on taxable amount
$1 million+	40%	$345,800 base tax + 40% on taxable amount

Practical Example:

Consider an estate valued at $14.05 million in 2024. The portion of the estate exceeding the $13.61 million exemption—$440,000—is subject to taxation. At the relevant tax tier, this results in a base tax payment, coupled with an additional marginal rate on the excess amount, culminating in a calculated estate tax obligation.

Strategies for Estate Tax Planning

Given the potential impact of federal estate taxes on an estate's value, employing strategies to mitigate this tax is a key component of estate planning. Options include making charitable contributions, leveraging annual gift exclusions, and considering strategic transfers that can reduce the taxable estate. Additionally, consulting with financial advisors can help you build strategies that align with specific estate planning goals, ensuring a legacy that reflects the grantor's intentions while optimizing tax outcomes.

The federal estate tax thresholds and rates for 2024 underscore the necessity for proactive and informed estate planning. By understanding these regulations and employing strategic planning, individuals can navigate the complexities of estate taxation, ensuring their legacy is preserved for future generations. Engaging with estate planning professionals can guide you in this process, offering peace of mind that one's financial legacy is secure.

Gift Taxes: Planning and Strategy

In the tapestry of estate planning, gift taxes represent a critical thread, weaving together the present actions of gifting with the future implications on one's estate. Understanding the intricacies of gift taxes and strategically employing gifting as a part of your estate planning can significantly impact the legacy you intend to leave behind. This section delves into the fundamentals of gift taxes, offering insights into effective planning and strategy.

The Basics of Gift Taxes

Gift taxes are federal taxes applied to the transfer of property or money to another individual without receiving something of equal value in return. The IRS mandates that any individual can give a certain amount to another individual each year without incurring gift taxes, known as the annual gift tax exclusion. For 2024, this exclusion amount is set at $18,000 per recipient. This means that you can give up to $18,000 to as many individuals as you like within a year without triggering the gift tax.

Lifetime Gift Tax Exemption

Beyond the annual exclusion, there's also a lifetime gift tax exemption, which is intricately linked to the estate tax exemption. This means that gifts exceeding the annual exclusion count towards the lifetime exemption limit, which mirrors the estate tax exemption amount. For 2024, this amount is $13.61 million. Strategic gifting can thus play a pivotal role in estate planning, allowing individuals to transfer wealth to their heirs while alive, potentially reducing the size of their estate and the corresponding estate taxes.

Strategic Gifting: Maximizing Impact

In the realm of estate planning, strategic gifting emerges as a potent tool, allowing individuals to manage their taxable estate while bestowing financial benefits to their loved ones during their lifetime. With the annual gift tax exclusion set at $18,000 per recipient in 2024, strategic gifting offers a pathway to reduce the taxable estate and leverage tax benefits effectively. Here's a deeper dive into how strategic gifting can be employed to maximize its impact.

Utilizing Annual Exclusions

The annual gift tax exclusion represents a foundational strategy in estate planning. By gifting up to $18,000 to any number of individuals each year, you can significantly decrease the size of your estate without incurring gift taxes or eating into your lifetime gift tax exemption. For couples, this strategy doubles in effectiveness, allowing gifts up to $36,000 per recipient when combining exclusions (In the context of estate and gift taxes, an "exclusion" refers to the amount that can be transferred without incurring any tax liability). This method serves not only to diminish the potential estate tax burden but also to incrementally transfer wealth, facilitating financial support or growth opportunities for beneficiaries now, rather than posthumously.

Paying for Medical and Educational Expenses

A nuanced but powerful aspect of strategic gifting lies in direct payments for medical and educational expenses. Payments made directly to an institution for someone else's medical bills or tuition fees do not count toward the $18,000 annual exclusion limit. This exclusion extends to encompass tuition payments for any level of education but does not cover other educational costs such as books, supplies, or room and board. Similarly, for medical expenses, the payment must be made directly to the care provider to qualify for exclusion. This avenue of gifting not only offers a way to support loved ones but also serves as an effective method to reduce the taxable estate.

Importance of Documenting Gifts

Documenting each gift that falls under the annual exclusion or other gifting strategies is paramount. Detailed records should include the amount, recipient, date of the gift, and the purpose if it qualifies for a specific exclusion (such as tuition or medical expenses). This documentation is crucial for accurately reporting gifts on tax returns when necessary and ensuring that your estate planning aligns with tax regulations. Maintaining comprehensive records aids in the strategic planning process, allowing for a clear overview of how gifting impacts the overall estate.

Planning Considerations and Timing

The strategic timing of gifts is a nuanced yet pivotal element of estate planning, directly influencing the taxable estate and the implications of gift taxes. Initiating gifting early in one's financial lifecycle and maintaining a consistent gifting strategy can lead to a considerable reduction in the taxable estate, effectively diminishing potential estate taxes at the time of death. This approach allows for a proactive redistribution of wealth, aligning with long-term estate planning objectives while benefiting loved ones during the grantor's lifetime.

The Role of Timing in Gifting

1. **Incremental Wealth Transfer**: By leveraging the annual gift tax exclusion, individuals can systematically transfer wealth to their beneficiaries, reducing the size of their estate over time. This methodical approach, when started early, can have compounding effects, significantly impacting the estate's taxable value.

2. **Market Considerations**: The timing of certain gifts, especially those involving securities or real estate, may be influenced by market conditions. Gifting assets when their market value is lower can maximize the impact of the exclusion and reduce the taxable estate more efficiently.

3. **Lifetime Events**: Major life events of beneficiaries, such as college enrollment or home purchases, present opportunities for strategic gifting that aligns with both the beneficiaries' needs and the grantor's estate planning goals.

4. **Balancing Generosity and Financial Security**: While gifting can play a crucial role in estate planning, it's essential to balance this strategy with the need for personal financial security. Ensuring that gifting does not undermine one's own lifestyle or financial needs is critical.

Collaborating with Professionals

Navigating the intricacies of gift taxes and their broader implications for estate planning demands a level of expertise that often extends beyond the layperson's purview. Collaboration with seasoned professionals—financial advisors, estate planning attorneys, and tax specialists—becomes indispensable.

Why Professional Guidance Matters

1. **Navigating Tax Laws**: Tax laws are complex and subject to change. Professionals stay abreast of these changes, providing guidance that ensures compliance and optimizes tax advantages.

2. **Customized Gifting Strategies**: Each estate is unique, necessitating personalized gifting strategies that reflect the specific circumstances and goals of the individual. Professionals can devise plans that are both efficient and tailored to personal objectives.

3. **Coordinating with Overall Estate Plans**: Gifting is one component of a comprehensive estate plan. Professionals ensure that gifting strategies complement other elements of the estate plan, such as trusts, wills, and healthcare directives, creating a cohesive approach to legacy planning.

4. **Mitigating Risks**: Experienced advisors can identify potential risks or pitfalls in gifting strategies, offering solutions to mitigate these issues and protect both the grantor's and beneficiaries' interests.

5. **Facilitating Complex Transactions**: Certain gifts, particularly those involving real estate or business interests, may require intricate legal and financial maneuvers. Professionals facilitate

these transactions, ensuring they are executed properly and in line with overall estate planning goals.

Reporting Requirements for Taxable Gifts

When navigating the complexities of gift taxes, understanding the reporting requirements for taxable gifts is crucial. The Internal Revenue Service (IRS) mandates the reporting of gifts that exceed the annual exclusion amount, currently set at $18,000 per recipient for 2024. This reporting is a critical aspect of the tax code designed to ensure transparency and compliance with federal tax laws. Here's a detailed exploration of the reporting requirements for taxable gifts.

Gifts Exceeding the Annual Exclusion

Any gift to an individual that surpasses the annual exclusion amount requires reporting to the IRS. So, If you give someone a gift that's worth more than the yearly allowed amount, you need to tell the IRS. But this doesn't mean you'll have to pay taxes right away. It just means the value of the gift over that yearly limit will be subtracted from a big, lifetime amount you're allowed to give away tax-free, which currently is $13.61 million.

Form 709: United States Gift (and Generation-Skipping Transfer) Tax Return

The primary document for reporting taxable gifts is Form 709: United States Gift (and Generation-Skipping Transfer) Tax Return. This form must be filed by anyone who gives gifts exceeding the annual exclusion limit to a single recipient within a calendar year. Form 709 allows the IRS to track the use of an individual's lifetime exemption against the gift and estate tax.

1. **When to File**: Form 709 is due by April 15 of the year following the year in which the taxable gifts were made. If more time is needed, the filer can request an extension to file the form, similar to the process for individual income tax returns.

2. **What to Include**: The form requires detailed information about each gift that exceeds the annual exclusion, including the recipient's name, the gift's value, and the date of the gift. It also asks for information on gifts that qualify for marital or charitable deductions, which are exempt from gift taxes despite exceeding the annual exclusion.

3. **Split Gifts Between Spouses**: If spouses elect to split gifts, effectively doubling their annual exclusion per recipient, both spouses must file Form 709, even if only one spouse made the actual gift. This ensures that the IRS is aware of each spouse's intention to split the gifts and properly tracks their lifetime exemptions.

Gift Tax Payment (If Applicable)

While the requirement to file Form 709 is triggered by gifts exceeding the annual exclusion, paying gift tax is relatively rare due to the substantial lifetime exemption. If the cumulative value of gifts over the annual exclusion amounts to more than the lifetime exemption, gift tax may be due. The tax rate ranges from 18% to 40%, depending on the amount above the exemption. However, most individuals structure their gifts to avoid depleting their lifetime exemption and incurring taxes.

Strategic Gifting and Reporting

Proper reporting of taxable gifts is a strategic component of estate planning, allowing individuals to manage their lifetime exemption and minimize potential estate taxes upon their death. By adhering to reporting requirements, individuals can make informed decisions about their gifting strategies, ensuring that they take full advantage of available exemptions and deductions to pass on their wealth efficiently.

Inheritance Taxes: State-Level Considerations

While the landscape of estate planning at the federal level focuses largely on estate taxes, navigating the intricacies of state-level taxation introduces another layer of complexity, particularly when it comes to inheritance taxes. Understanding the distinction between inheritance and estate taxes, as well as the specific rules and rates that apply at the state level, is crucial for effective estate planning and ensuring a smooth transfer of assets to beneficiaries.

The Distinction Between Inheritance and Estate Taxes

Inheritance and estate taxes, though often mentioned in the same breath, are distinct in who they tax and how they are levied.

- **Estate Taxes** are deducted from the deceased's entire estate before distribution to the heirs. This tax is based on the net value of all the assets owned by the deceased at the time of their death. Estate taxes can be levied at both the federal and state levels, though not all states impose an estate tax.
- **Inheritance Taxes**, on the other hand, are imposed on the beneficiaries who receive assets from the estate. Unlike estate taxes, inheritance taxes are paid by the beneficiaries, and the rates can vary depending on the relationship between the beneficiary and the deceased. The closer the familial relationship, the lower the tax rate, with spouses often exempt and distant relatives or non-relatives facing higher rates.

State-Level Inheritance Taxes

Only a handful of states impose an inheritance tax, and the rules, rates, and exemptions vary significantly from one state to another. States that do levy an inheritance tax include Iowa, Kentucky, Maryland, Nebraska, New Jersey, and Pennsylvania. Each of these states has its own set of guidelines determining how the inheritance tax is calculated, who is exempt, and at what rate the tax is applied.

For example, in some states, transfers to surviving spouses are entirely exempt from inheritance tax, while transfers to children and grandchildren may be taxed at a reduced rate. Conversely, transfers to siblings, nieces, nephews, or unrelated individuals may attract higher rates of taxation.

Navigating State-Level Considerations for Inheritance Taxes

Understanding and planning for state-level inheritance taxes requires a nuanced approach, given the variability in tax laws from one state to another. Each state that imposes an inheritance tax has its own set of rules regarding rates, exemptions, and which beneficiaries are taxed. This variability necessitates a detailed strategy tailored to the specific circumstances of an estate and its beneficiaries, particularly when assets are spread across multiple states or when beneficiaries reside in different jurisdictions. Here's a deeper dive into navigating these state-level considerations.

Familiarize Yourself with State Laws

The first step in effectively navigating state-level considerations is to become familiar with the inheritance tax laws of the state(s) in which the estate holds assets and where the beneficiaries reside. This includes understanding:

- **Exemption Thresholds**: Some states offer exemptions based on the relationship to the decedent, with spouses and direct descendants often receiving the most favorable treatment.
- **Tax Rates**: Inheritance tax rates can vary widely, not only from state to state but also based on the beneficiary's relation to the decedent and the value of the inheritance.
- **Filing Requirements**: Knowing when and how to file for inheritance taxes, including deadlines and necessary documentation, is crucial to avoid penalties.

Strategic Asset Distribution

Once you have a thorough understanding of the relevant state laws, consider how assets might be distributed to minimize inheritance tax liabilities. Strategies may include:

- **Directing Assets to Exempt Beneficiaries**: If certain beneficiaries, like spouses or children, are exempt from inheritance taxes in the decedent's state, it might make sense to allocate more assets to them.
- **Equalizing Inheritances Through Gifts**: If planning to leave assets to non-exempt beneficiaries, consider using the annual gift tax exclusion to gradually transfer wealth to these individuals during your lifetime, thereby reducing the size of the taxable estate.

Utilizing Trusts

Trusts can be a powerful tool in estate planning, offering a way to manage how and when beneficiaries receive their inheritance, which can affect their inheritance tax liability. Consider:

- **Bypass Trusts**: For married couples, a bypass trust can help utilize both spouses' exemptions fully, potentially doubling the amount that can be passed on tax-free.
- **Dynasty Trusts**: These can protect assets from taxes and creditors over multiple generations, depending on state law.

Life Insurance as a Strategic Tool

Life insurance proceeds are typically exempt from inheritance taxes and can be used strategically within an estate plan:

- **Paying Inheritance Taxes**: Beneficiaries can use life insurance proceeds to pay any inheritance taxes due, preserving the value of the estate.
- **Equalizing Inheritances**: Life insurance can deliver liquidity to equalize inheritances among beneficiaries, particularly if the estate consists largely of illiquid assets like real estate or a family business.

Professional Guidance is Key

Given the complexity of navigating state-level inheritance taxes, engaging with estate planning professionals—attorneys, tax advisors, and financial planners—who have expertise in the relevant state laws is invaluable. These professionals can:

- **Offer Customized Advice**: Tailored strategies can be developed to address your specific estate planning goals and the unique challenges presented by state-level inheritance taxes.
- **Stay Updated on Law Changes**: Tax laws are subject to change, and professionals can help you stay compliant and make adjustments to your estate plan as necessary.

Income Taxes and the Estate

In the realm of estate planning, managing income taxes for the estate itself is a crucial component that often requires meticulous attention. Beyond the more commonly discussed estate and inheritance taxes, the decedent's estate may also be responsible for income taxes. This includes filing the final income tax return for the deceased, as well as handling any ongoing tax obligations the estate may incur during the administration period. This chapter explores the key aspects of income taxes related to estates, focusing primarily on the filing requirements for the deceased's final tax return.

Filing the Deceased's Final Income Tax Return

The responsibility of filing a final income tax return for the deceased falls to the estate's executor or administrator. This final return covers the period from January 1st of the year of death until the date of death. Here's a breakdown of what this entails:

1. **Gathering Information**: The executor must compile all necessary financial information to accurately report the deceased's income up to the date of death. This includes wages, dividends, interest income, and any other sources of income.

2. **Deductions and Credits**: Just like any other tax return, the final return for the deceased can include deductions and credits for which they were eligible. This might include medical expenses, administrative expenses (such as legal and accounting fees), charitable contributions made before death, and personal exemptions.

3. **Filing Status**: The filing status on the final return will depend on the deceased's marital status at the time of death. If married, the surviving spouse may file a joint return for the year of death.

4. **Due Date**: The final tax return is due by the standard filing deadline of April 15th in the year following the individual's death. If more time is needed, the executor can request an extension.

5. **Reporting to Beneficiaries**: If the estate generates income after the date of death, beneficiaries may need to be informed of any income that could be taxable to them on their personal tax returns.

Estate Income Taxes (Form 1041)

Apart from the final personal income tax return, the estate itself may need to file an income tax return if it generates income during the administration period. This is separate from the estate tax and applies to income earned by the estate after the decedent's death. The filing requirements are as follows:

1. **Threshold for Filing**: An estate must file Form 1041, U.S. Income Tax Return for Estates and Trusts, if its gross income for the tax year is $600 or more.

2. **Taxable Income**: The estate's taxable income includes interest, dividends, and other income earned on the estate's assets. Expenses incurred during the administration of the estate, such as legal fees, executor's fees, and other administrative costs, can be deducted.

3. **Filing Deadline**: Form 1041 is due by April 15th for the previous tax year. Extensions can be requested if additional time is needed.

Planning and Coordination

Effectively managing the income tax obligations of the deceased and their estate requires careful planning and coordination:

1. **Professional Assistance**: Engaging a tax professional experienced in estate administration can ensure compliance with tax laws and optimize the estate's tax position.

2. **Communication with Beneficiaries**: Keeping beneficiaries informed about the estate's income and any potential tax implications for them is essential for transparency and planning purposes.

3. **Estate Planning Integration**: Consideration of potential estate income taxes should be integrated into broader estate planning strategies to minimize tax liabilities and maximize the value passed to beneficiaries.

The Concept of "Income in Respect of a Decedent" (IRD)

IRD refers to income that the decedent was entitled to receive during their lifetime but was not actually received before their death, thereby not included in the final income tax return. Understanding IRD is crucial for both executors and beneficiaries, as it affects how the estate and the subsequent income received by beneficiaries are taxed.

Nature and Examples of IRD

IRD can encompass a variety of income types, including but not limited to:

1. **Outstanding Salaries, Bonuses, or Commissions**: Earnings that were earned by the decedent but not paid prior to death.

2. **Deferred Compensation**: Income from retirement plans, IRAs, or other deferred compensation plans that the decedent had rights to but had not yet received.

3. **Unpaid Dividends and Interest**: Income from investments that was declared but not paid before the decedent's death.

4. **Sales Proceeds**: Proceeds from sales under contract but not completed by the time of death.

Tax Implications of IRD Simplified

When an estate or beneficiaries receive Income in Respect of a Decedent (IRD), they must pay income tax on it. This rule ensures that the income, which the decedent did not receive while alive, is taxed after their death. An important point is that IRD might be taxed twice: once as income to whoever receives it and again as part of the estate's overall value, affecting estate taxes. To lessen the burden of this potential double taxation, there are special tax breaks and deductions:

- **Estate Tax Deduction**: If you're a beneficiary receiving IRD, you might get to deduct a part of the estate tax that relates to the IRD's value from your income taxes. This doesn't lower the estate's value for estate tax calculations, but it can reduce the income tax you owe.

- **Itemizing Deductions**: To use the estate tax deduction for IRD on your taxes, you need to choose to itemize deductions on your tax return. This choice could change how you decide to file your taxes.

These rules are designed to offer some tax relief for IRD, making the process fairer for beneficiaries handling this specific type of income.

Managing IRD in Estate Planning

Effective management of IRD in estate planning and administration requires careful consideration and strategic actions:

- **Identification and Tracking**: Executors and trustees should identify potential sources of IRD early in the estate administration process and track these items separately to ensure proper tax treatment.

- **Informing Beneficiaries**: Beneficiaries should be informed about the nature of IRD they receive and the associated tax implications, including the possibility of an estate tax deduction.

- **Professional Consultation**: Given the complexities surrounding IRD and its impact on estate and income taxes, consulting with tax professionals and estate planners is advisable. These experts can provide guidance on handling IRD, optimizing tax outcomes, and integrating IRD considerations into broader estate planning strategies.

Capital Gains Tax Considerations

In the context of estate planning and inheritance, capital gains tax plays a significant role in determining the financial impact on inherited assets. Understanding how capital gains tax applies to these assets can help beneficiaries make informed decisions about managing or disposing of their inheritance. Here's a detailed look at the impact of capital gains tax on inherited assets and strategies to navigate these tax implications.

Impact of Capital Gains Tax on Inherited Assets

Capital gains tax is levied on the profit from the sale of assets such as stocks, bonds, real estate, and other investments. The key factor distinguishing inherited assets is the concept of "step-up in basis," which significantly affects the calculation of capital gains tax.

- **Step-Up in Basis**: Generally, when you inherit assets, their tax basis is "stepped up" to their fair market value (FMV) as of the decedent's date of death. This means if the assets have appreciated in value over the decedent's ownership period, the beneficiaries' basis for calculating capital gains tax will be the value at the time of the decedent's death, not what the decedent originally paid for the assets.

- For example, if a decedent purchased stock for $10,000 (original basis) and it was worth $50,000 at the time of their death, the beneficiary's basis in the stock would be stepped up to

$50,000. If the beneficiary later sells the stock for $55,000, they would only be taxed on the $5,000 gain, not the $45,000 gain from the decedent's original purchase price.

- **No Capital Gains Tax Due at Time of Inheritance**: Beneficiaries do not owe capital gains tax simply because they inherit assets. The tax only applies if and when the inherited assets are sold and there is a gain based on the stepped-up basis.

Planning and Strategy

1. **Evaluating the Sale of Inherited Assets**: Beneficiaries should carefully consider the timing of selling inherited assets. Understanding the stepped-up basis can guide decisions to sell assets that have appreciated significantly since the decedent's purchase, potentially minimizing capital gains tax.

2. **Holding Period**: For capital gains tax purposes, inherited assets are always considered long-term, regardless of how long the beneficiary actually holds them before selling. Long-term capital gains are taxed at lower rates than short-term gains, providing a tax advantage to beneficiaries.

3. **Consulting with Tax Professionals**: Given the complexities of capital gains tax and the step-up in basis, beneficiaries are encouraged to consult with tax professionals. They can give advice on managing inherited assets, optimizing tax implications, and incorporating these assets into the beneficiary's broader financial plan.

The impact of capital gains tax on inherited assets underscores the importance of strategic planning for both estate executors and beneficiaries. The step-up in basis provides a significant tax benefit, potentially reducing the capital gains tax liability on the sale of appreciated assets inherited from a decedent. By understanding these rules and working with financial advisors or tax professionals, beneficiaries can make informed decisions that align with their financial goals and minimize tax liabilities.

Retirement Accounts and Tax Implications

Tax Treatment of Inherited Retirement Accounts (IRA, 401(k), etc.)

Inherited retirement accounts, such as Individual Retirement Accounts (IRAs) and 401(k)s, are a common element of many estates. The tax treatment of these accounts when passed on to beneficiaries is complex and varies significantly based on the type of account, the relationship of the beneficiary to the decedent, and recent changes in legislation. Understanding these nuances is crucial for both estate planners and beneficiaries to ensure tax-efficient management and distribution of these assets.

Types of Retirement Accounts and Their Tax Implications

- **Traditional IRA and 401(k) Accounts**: Money put into these accounts isn't taxed upfront, meaning you don't pay taxes on the amount you contribute at the time you put it in. But, when you or someone who inherits the account takes money out, that money is taxed like regular income. The amount of tax paid depends on how much the person taking the money out earns that year.

- **Roth IRA and Roth 401(k) Accounts**: These accounts are a bit different because the money you put in has already been taxed. So, the money grows in the account without being taxed again, and when it's taken out, it's tax-free, as long as the account has been open for at least five years. This is great for people who inherit these accounts because they don't have to pay taxes on withdrawals.

The Secure Act and Its Impact

The Setting Every Community Up for Retirement Enhancement (SECURE) Act, enacted in December 2019, made significant changes to the rules governing inherited retirement accounts. One of the most notable changes is the elimination of the "stretch IRA" provision for most non-spouse beneficiaries, replacing it with a 10-year rule for the full distribution of the account:

- **10-Year Rule**: Most non-spouse beneficiaries are now required to fully distribute the inherited retirement account's assets within ten years following the year of the account owner's death. This rule applies regardless of the account type and does not require annual minimum distributions, allowing beneficiaries some flexibility in planning distributions for tax efficiency.

- **Exceptions**: Spouses, minor children (until they reach the age of majority), disabled individuals, chronically ill individuals, and beneficiaries not more than ten years younger than the decedent are generally exempt from the 10-year rule and can take distributions over their life expectancy.

Considering Tax Implications for Beneficiaries

Beneficiaries inheriting retirement accounts should consider several tax-related factors:

- **Timing of Distributions**: The timing of withdrawals from inherited traditional IRAs or 401(k)s can significantly impact the beneficiary's tax liability, especially under the 10-year distribution rule. Strategically planning distributions can help manage tax burdens more effectively.

- **State Taxes**: In addition to federal income taxes, beneficiaries should be aware of any state income taxes that may apply to distributions from inherited retirement accounts.

- **Rollovers**: Spouse beneficiaries have the option to perform a spousal rollover, transferring the inherited assets into their own IRA, potentially deferring taxes and required distributions until they reach the age of 72.

The tax treatment of inherited retirement accounts encompasses a complex set of rules that can significantly impact beneficiaries' tax liabilities. The SECURE Act's introduction, with its 10-year distribution rule, necessitates careful planning and consideration by beneficiaries to manage tax implications efficiently. Consulting with financial advisors and tax professionals can guide you, helping beneficiaries navigate these challenges and make informed decisions about their inherited retirement assets.

Required Minimum Distributions (RMDs) and Their Impact on Beneficiaries

Required Minimum Distributions (RMDs) are a key concept in the realm of retirement accounts, affecting both account holders and their beneficiaries. Understanding RMDs is crucial for anyone inheriting a retirement account, as they dictate the timing and amount of withdrawals, thereby influencing the tax implications for beneficiaries.

What are RMDs?

RMDs are the minimum amounts that the IRS requires to be withdrawn annually from retirement accounts after the account holder reaches a certain age or upon the account holder's death when passed to a non-spouse beneficiary. The purpose behind RMDs is to ensure that the tax-advantaged savings in these accounts are eventually taxed, rather than being allowed to grow tax-deferred indefinitely.

Impact on Beneficiaries

1. **Traditional IRA and 401(k) Accounts**: Beneficiaries of these accounts are subject to RMDs, which are taxed as ordinary income at the beneficiary's current tax rate. The amount of the RMD is determined by the IRS's life expectancy tables and the account's total value at the end of the previous year.

2. **Roth IRA and Roth 401(k) Accounts**: While Roth accounts do not require RMDs for the original account holder, beneficiaries of these accounts are subject to RMD rules. However, the distributions from inherited Roth accounts are generally tax-free, provided the original account was opened at least five years before the distributions are taken.

Strategies for Managing RMDs

Beneficiaries should consider several strategies to manage the impact of RMDs:

- **Timing Withdrawals**: Especially under the 10-year rule, planning the timing of withdrawals to spread out tax liabilities can be beneficial. Beneficiaries might choose to take larger distributions in years when they expect lower personal income.

- **Understanding Tax Implications**: Consulting with a tax advisor to understand the tax implications of RMDs can help beneficiaries make informed decisions and potentially identify ways to minimize their tax burden.
- **Consider the Entire Financial Picture**: Beneficiaries should consider RMDs in the context of their overall financial situation, including other income sources and tax considerations, to make strategic decisions about withdrawals.

RMDs from inherited retirement accounts are a critical factor that beneficiaries must navigate carefully. These rules determine not only when money must be withdrawn but also have significant tax implications. By understanding the specifics of RMDs, including recent changes under the SECURE Act, beneficiaries can make informed decisions that optimize their financial and tax situation, ultimately affecting the value they derive from their inherited retirement assets.

Trusts and Tax Planning

Revocable vs. Irrevocable Trusts - Tax Implications

Trusts are a cornerstone of sophisticated estate planning, offering flexibility, control, and potential tax advantages. Understanding the tax implications of revocable and irrevocable trusts is crucial for effectively incorporating them into an estate plan. Each type has distinct characteristics that affect how it's taxed and managed, influencing the overall strategy for estate and tax planning.

Revocable Trusts

Also known as living trusts, they are flexible estate planning tools that allow the grantor (the person who creates the trust) to retain control over the assets within it. The grantor has the ability to alter, amend, or revoke the trust at any time during their lifetime.

- **Tax Implications**: For tax purposes, revocable trusts are generally considered transparent. This means that all income generated by the trust's assets is taxable to the grantor, as the IRS views these assets as still being under the grantor's direct control. Income from the trust is reported on the grantor's personal income tax returns, and the trust itself is not subject to separate taxation. Upon the grantor's death, the trust typically becomes irrevocable, and its tax implications may change accordingly.

A Practical Example

Scenario: John creates a revocable trust and transfers his rental property into it. He retains the right to revoke it and manages the property as the trustee, collecting rent and paying expenses related to the property.

Tax Implications: Since the trust is revocable, John continues to report all rental income and expenses on his personal income tax return, just as he did before transferring the property into the trust. The IRS views the trust's assets as still under John's control, so the trust itself is not taxed separately.

Irrevocable Trusts

Unlike revocable trusts, irrevocable ones cannot be altered or revoked by the grantor once they are established. This transfer of control and ownership of the trust's assets has significant tax implications.

- **Tax Implications**: Irrevocable trusts are treated as separate tax entities. They are responsible for their own tax filings and can be subject to income tax, estate tax, and gift tax under certain conditions. Income generated by the trust's assets that is not distributed to beneficiaries is taxed at the trust level, often at higher rates than individual rates. However, distributions to beneficiaries are generally taxed at the beneficiary's individual income tax rate. Irrevocable trusts can be structured to achieve specific tax advantages, such as charitable giving or wealth transfer strategies that minimize estate taxes.

A Practical Example

Scenario: Maria establishes an irrevocable trust, transferring her investment portfolio into it. She appoints her brother as the trustee and her children as beneficiaries. The trust stipulates that the income generated by the investments is to be distributed annually to her children.

Tax Implications: The trust is now a separate entity for tax purposes. It files its own tax return and pays taxes on any income not distributed to the beneficiaries. The distributed income is taxed to Maria's children at their individual tax rates. Since Maria cannot change the trust, the assets are removed from her taxable estate, potentially reducing estate taxes upon her death.

The Role of Grantor Trusts in Estate Planning

Grantor trusts once set up, can't be changed (irrevocable). But, there's a twist: any money the trust makes is treated as the income of the person who set up the trust (the grantor), for tax reasons. This setup has some benefits:

- **Income Tax**: Even though the trust owns the assets, any money it makes is reported on the grantor's tax return. This can be helpful because the grantor might use certain tax breaks or deductions to lower their tax bill based on this income.
- **Estate Tax Benefits**: When someone puts their assets into a grantor trust, those assets are no longer counted as part of their personal estate. This means when the grantor passes away their estate might owe less in taxes, leaving more for their heirs.

In simple terms, grantor trusts let the person who creates the trust keep paying taxes on the trust's income, which can lead to tax savings now and in the future.

A Practical Example

Scenario: Alex sets up an irrevocable grantor trust, funding it with a mix of stocks and bonds. Despite its irrevocable nature, the trust contains provisions that make all of its income taxable to Alex.

Tax Implications: Although the trust is irrevocable, Alex reports all income generated by the trust's assets on his personal tax return, paying the taxes due. This setup allows the trust's assets to grow tax-free, benefiting the beneficiaries. Furthermore, because the trust is considered outside of Alex's estate, it reduces his overall estate value for estate tax purposes.

Utilizing Trusts for Charitable Giving and Tax Deductions

Trusts offer a versatile avenue for charitable giving, providing not only a way to support causes and organizations important to the grantor but also potential tax benefits that can enhance the financial efficiency of one's estate plan. Understanding how to leverage trusts for charitable purposes involves a grasp of what charitable giving entails and the specific types of trusts designed for this purpose.

What is Charitable Giving?

Charitable giving refers to the act of donating resources, including money, goods, or time, to nonprofit organizations or causes with the aim of supporting societal, environmental, cultural, or educational initiatives. In the context of estate planning, charitable giving often takes a financial form, with individuals allocating part of their estate to charity either during their lifetime or upon their death. This form of giving not only furthers the philanthropic goals of the donor but can also provide significant tax advantages.

Trusts and Charitable Giving

Trusts can be strategically used to structure charitable giving in a way that maximizes tax benefits while ensuring the donor's philanthropic objectives are met. Two primary types of trusts used in charitable giving are Charitable Remainder Trusts (CRTs) and Charitable Lead Trusts (CLTs).

- **Charitable Remainder Trusts (CRTs)**: A CRT is an irrevocable trust that provides an income stream to non-charitable beneficiaries (such as the grantor or family members) for a period, after which the remaining assets are donated to designated charitable organizations. The grantor receives a tax deduction based on the present value of the assets that will eventually go to charity, potentially reducing income and estate taxes. This setup benefits the grantor and their heirs by providing income and tax savings, while also ensuring a future gift to charity.

- **Charitable Lead Trusts (CLTs)**: In contrast to CRTs, CLTs first allocate income to one or more charitable organizations for a set period, after which the remainder of the trust assets passes to non-charitable beneficiaries, such as the grantor's heirs. CLTs can offer estate or gift tax deductions based on the value of the income stream given to charity, reducing the taxable value of the assets transferred to heirs. This type of trust appeals to individuals looking to support charity immediately while still preserving assets for future generations.

Tax Deductions and Benefits

The tax implications of utilizing trusts for charitable giving are significant and multifaceted:

- **Immediate Tax Deductions**: Both CRTs and CLTs can provide the grantor with immediate tax deductions for the charitable portion of the trust, calculated based on IRS formulas that consider factors like the term of the trust, projected income, and current interest rates.

- **Estate Tax Reduction**: By removing assets from the estate and directing them toward charitable causes, these trusts can reduce the size of the grantor's taxable estate, potentially leading to lower estate taxes upon the grantor's death.

- **Avoidance of Capital Gains Tax**: If appreciated assets are transferred into a charitable trust, the sale of these assets within the trust does not trigger capital gains taxes, allowing the full value of the assets to benefit the trust's beneficiaries and charitable causes.

Utilizing trusts for charitable giving offers a strategic method to achieve philanthropic goals while reaping significant tax benefits. By carefully selecting the type of trust and understanding the associated tax implications, donors can support charitable causes, provide for their beneficiaries, and optimize the tax efficiency of their estate. Given the complexity of these arrangements, consulting with legal and financial professionals specialized in charitable giving and trusts is essential to ensure that such strategies are implemented effectively and aligned with broader estate planning objectives.

The Use of Donor-Advised Funds (DAFs) in Estate Planning

Donor-Advised Funds (DAFs) have emerged as a popular and flexible tool for philanthropic efforts within estate planning. These funds offer individuals a way to make charitable contributions over time, receive immediate tax benefits, and maintain advisory privileges over how contributions are disbursed to charitable organizations. Understanding how DAFs can be integrated into estate planning offers a comprehensive approach to managing charitable giving and leveraging associated tax advantages.

What Are Donor-Advised Funds?

A Donor-Advised Fund is a philanthropic vehicle administered by a public charity. It allows donors to make a charitable contribution to the fund, receive an immediate tax deduction, and then recommend grants from the fund to qualified nonprofit organizations over time. DAFs serve as an intermediary step between the donor and the ultimate charitable beneficiaries, offering an organized, flexible way to manage charitable giving.

Benefits of DAFs in Estate Planning

- **Get Tax Benefits Now**: When you put money into a DAF, you can get a tax break right away, in the same year you make the contribution. This is really helpful, especially if you've made a lot of money that year, because it can lower your taxes.
- **Lower Estate Taxes Later**: By putting your assets into a DAF, you're essentially moving them out of your estate. This means when it's time to calculate estate taxes, your estate could be smaller and possibly owe less tax. Plus, you still get to support your favorite charities.
- **Easy and Flexible Giving**: DAFs make giving to charity really easy. You don't have to deal with all the paperwork or decide right away where all the money should go. You can take your time and choose which charities to support as you go along.
- **Pass on Your Values**: You can use a DAF to teach your family about giving by having them help decide how to distribute the money, even after you're gone. It's a way to keep your charitable spirit alive through future generations.
- **Give Anonymously**: If you want, you can give money to charities without having your name attached. DAFs let you make anonymous donations, so you can support causes you care about quietly.

Integrating DAFs into Your Estate Plan

To effectively incorporate DAFs into your estate plan, consider the following steps:

- **Strategic Contribution Timing**: Align contributions to DAFs with your overall financial and tax planning strategy, taking advantage of tax deductions in high-income years or when you have highly appreciated assets that can be donated to minimize capital gains taxes.
- **Define Philanthropic Goals**: Clearly outline your philanthropic objectives and how you wish your contributions to be used, both during your lifetime and as part of your legacy. This can guide the selection of charities and the timing of distributions.
- **Coordinate with Other Estate Planning Tools**: Ensure that your DAF strategy complements other elements of your estate plan, such as trusts, wills, and direct charitable bequests, for a cohesive approach to your philanthropic and financial legacy.
- **Consult with Professionals**: Work with estate planning attorneys and financial advisors familiar with DAFs to tailor your contributions and succession plans according to your estate planning goals.

Donor-Advised Funds offer a powerful and flexible option for integrating charitable giving into estate planning. By leveraging DAFs, individuals can achieve immediate tax benefits, engage in strategic philanthropy, and reduce their estate tax liability, all while establishing a lasting philanthropic legacy. Careful planning and professional guidance are key to maximizing the benefits of DAFs within the broader context of estate planning.

Special Considerations for Business Owners in Estate Planning

For business owners, estate planning transcends the personal; it is an essential safeguard for the continuity and legacy of their life's work. Unlike traditional estate planning, which primarily focuses on personal assets, wills, and healthcare directives, business owners face a complex set of challenges that demand strategic foresight and meticulous planning. This chapter aims to shed light on the unique considerations business owners must navigate to ensure that their estate plan adequately protects both their personal and business interests.

The significance of estate planning for business owners cannot be overstated. A well-structured estate plan ensures that the business you have built continues to thrive, even in your absence, by providing clear directives on succession, asset distribution, and tax implications. It also offers peace of mind, knowing that your family's financial future is secure and that the legacy of your entrepreneurial spirit will endure.

However, the path to effective estate planning for business owners is fraught with complexities. The value of your business, its structure, and your long-term goals for succession and legacy all have essential roles in shaping your estate plan. Additionally, the intertwining of personal and business assets adds another layer of consideration, making it imperative to approach estate planning with a comprehensive and tailored strategy.

We'll explore the essential elements of estate planning unique to business owners, including business valuation, understanding the impact of different business structures, succession planning, tax considerations, asset protection, and planning for incapacity. By delving into these areas, I aim to provide business owners with the insights and tools necessary to navigate the estate planning process effectively, ensuring the protection and continuation of both their personal and business legacies.

As we embark on this exploration, remember that the goal of estate planning is not just to prepare for the inevitable but to create a roadmap that guides your business and your loved ones through the future, safeguarding the fruits of your hard work and vision. Estate planning for business owners is an investment in the future—a testament to your commitment to your business, your family, and the values you hold dear.

For business owners, the valuation of their business is a critical first step in the estate planning process. It sets the foundation for determining potential estate taxes, structuring succession plans, and ensuring fair and equitable asset distribution among heirs. Understanding how business valuation works, the factors that influence it, and its impact on estate planning is essential for any business owner looking to secure their legacy and protect their interests.

The Importance of Accurate Business Valuation

1. **Estate Tax Implications**: The value of your business significantly impacts the overall value of your estate, affecting estate tax liabilities. An accurate valuation is crucial for calculating potential estate taxes and exploring strategies to minimize them.

2. **Succession Planning**: Knowing the value of your business aids in making informed decisions about succession. Whether you plan to pass the business to family members, sell it to a partner, or explore other exit strategies, a clear understanding of its worth is paramount.

3. **Asset Distribution**: For business owners with multiple heirs, ensuring equitable distribution of assets can be challenging. A precise business valuation helps in devising a fair plan, especially when some heirs are more involved in the business than others.

Methods of Business Valuation

Several methods can be employed to value a business, each with its own set of considerations:

- **Asset-Based Approach**: This method calculates the net value of the business's assets minus its liabilities. It's straightforward but may not capture the full value of a profitable, ongoing concern.

- **Income Approach**: Often used for businesses with a strong earnings record, this approach forecasts future income and discounts it to present value. It's useful for businesses with significant growth potential.

- **Market Approach**: This method compares the business to similar companies that have been sold recently, providing a market-based perspective on value. It's particularly relevant in industries with active business sales.

The Role of Professionals in Business Valuation

Given the complexities involved in valuing a business, engaging with professional valuators or financial analysts is often necessary. These experts can:

1. **Provide an Objective Valuation**: Professionals bring an unbiased perspective to the valuation process, ensuring that the figure reflects the true market value of the business.

2. **Use Sophisticated Tools and Methods**: Experts have access to advanced tools and databases to analyze financial data, industry trends, and comparable sales, offering a comprehensive valuation.

3. **Navigate Legal and Tax Implications**: Professional valuators understand the legal and tax ramifications of different valuation methods, helping to position the business favorably for estate planning purposes.

Updating the Valuation

Business valuation is not a one-time task. Regular updates are crucial as the business grows, market conditions change, and new assets or liabilities emerge. These updates ensure that your estate plan remains aligned with the current value of your business, adjusting for fluctuations that could impact your estate's tax liabilities and succession plans.

Business Structure and Its Implications

Choosing the right structure for a business is a critical decision for any entrepreneur. This choice not only impacts the daily operations and legal liabilities of the business but also has significant implications for estate planning. The structure determines how ownership is transferred, the extent of personal liability, and tax obligations, all of which are pivotal considerations in planning for the future of both the business and the owner's estate.

Overview of Common Business Structures

- **Sole Proprietorship**: The simplest form, where one individual owns and operates the business. In estate planning, the business assets and liabilities are indistinguishable from the owner's personal assets, directly affecting the estate's value and liabilities.

- **Partnership**: Involves two or more individuals owning the business. Estate planning complexities arise in understanding how each partner's share can be transferred upon death and the implications for the surviving partners.

- **Limited Liability Company (LLC)**: Offers flexibility and protects owners (members) from personal liability. For estate planning, members must consider how their interest in the LLC is transferred, often governed by the operating agreement.

- **Corporation (C Corp and S Corp)**: Corporations are separate legal entities, providing the strongest protection against personal liability. Shareholder agreements play a crucial role in estate planning, detailing the transferability of shares.

Estate Planning Considerations by Structure

- **Transferability of Ownership**: The ease with which business ownership can be transferred upon the owner's death varies significantly by structure. Trusts, buy-sell agreements, and operating agreements are tools that can facilitate this transfer, with nuances depending on the business form.

- **Tax Implications**: The business structure influences the tax treatment of the business at both the operational and estate levels. For example, C Corps are subject to double taxation (corporate and dividend taxes), which affects estate valuation, while S Corps and LLCs offer pass-through taxation, directly impacting the owner's estate.
- **Continuity and Succession**: Planning for the continuity of the business after the owner's death is impacted by its structure. Sole proprietorships may cease to exist, whereas corporations and LLCs offer perpetual existence. The structure informs the development of a succession plan that aligns with the owner's estate planning goals.
- **Liability and Asset Protection**: The degree to which an owner's personal assets are protected from business liabilities varies with the structure, directly affecting estate risk. Incorporating or forming an LLC can protect personal assets, which is a significant consideration in safeguarding the value of the estate for heirs.

Strategic Use of Agreements in Estate Planning

- **Buy-Sell Agreements**: Especially important in partnerships and corporations, these agreements dictate how an owner's interest in the business is bought out upon death, ensuring business continuity and providing the estate with liquidity.
- **Operating Agreements for LLCs**: Detail how a member's interest is transferred upon death, crucial for ensuring that the member's estate planning wishes are honored.
- **Shareholder Agreements for Corporations**: Govern the transferability of shares, including any restrictions that might affect the estate's ability to sell or transfer shares.

The structure of a business has profound implications for estate planning, affecting everything from how ownership is transferred to the tax implications and the protection of personal assets. Business owners must carefully consider these implications when choosing a structure and planning for the future. Consulting with legal and financial professionals to navigate these considerations is essential, ensuring that the chosen structure not only supports the business's current success but also aligns with the owner's long-term estate planning objectives.

Succession Planning

Succession planning is a critical component of estate planning for business owners, ensuring that the business can continue to thrive and support beneficiaries long after the owner's departure. This process involves identifying and preparing new leaders to take over the business, thus safeguarding the owner's legacy and the company's future. Effective succession planning requires foresight, strategic thinking, and careful consideration of legal, financial, and emotional factors.

Understanding Succession Planning

- **Definition**: Succession planning is the process of identifying and developing new leaders who can replace old leaders when they leave, retire, or pass away. It's about ensuring the continuity of the business and preserving its value for future generations or sale.

- **Importance**: Without a clear succession plan, businesses face uncertainty and risk upon the owner's death or incapacity, potentially leading to operational disruptions, loss of value, or even the business's dissolution. A well-crafted plan provides stability, clear direction, and peace of mind for all stakeholders involved.

Key Components of Succession Planning

1. **Identifying Potential Successors**: This involves considering family members active in the business, key employees, or external candidates who have the skills and vision to lead the company forward. The decision should align with the company's long-term goals and the owner's estate planning objectives.

2. **Training and Development**: Once potential successors are identified, a development plan should be put in place to equip them with the necessary skills and knowledge. This might include leadership training, mentorship programs, and hands-on experience in various aspects of the business.

3. **Legal and Financial Considerations**: Succession planning must be integrated with the owner's broader estate plan, involving the transfer of ownership shares, restructuring of the business, and ensuring financial stability through the transition. Tools such as buy-sell agreements, trusts, and insurance policies can play critical roles.

4. **Communication**: Open and clear communication with family members, employees, and other stakeholders is essential to manage expectations, prevent conflicts, and ensure a smooth transition. This includes discussing the plan's details, the rationale behind successor selection and how the plan fits into the owner's estate planning goals.

Strategies for Succession Planning

- **Family Succession**: For many business owners, passing the business to the next generation is a priority. This requires careful planning to address family dynamics, equitable distribution of assets, and preparation of heirs to take on leadership roles.

- **Selling the Business**: Some owners may opt to sell the business, either to internal employees, competitors, or third parties. In such cases, succession planning focuses on maximizing the business's value, negotiating sale terms, and integrating the proceeds into the owner's estate plan.

- **Contingency Planning for Unforeseen Events**: Beyond long-term succession, it's important to have a contingency plan for sudden events like the owner's unexpected death or incapacity. This includes having interim leadership solutions and clear directives for immediate actions.

Succession planning is an indispensable element of comprehensive estate planning for business owners. It not only ensures the continuity of the business after the owner's departure but also aligns with the broader goals of preserving the owner's legacy and securing the financial future of the beneficiaries.

Strategic Tax Planning for Business Owners

For business owners, strategic tax planning is not just about compliance; it's a crucial component of maximizing profitability, ensuring business growth, and safeguarding a financial legacy. This comprehensive approach involves understanding the interplay between business operations, personal financial goals, and the evolving tax landscape to make informed decisions that optimize tax liabilities.

Understanding the Tax Landscape

Tax planning for business owners requires a deep dive into both personal and business taxes, including income tax, capital gains tax, estate tax, and potentially others depending on the business structure. The aim is to leverage tax credits, deductions, and favorable tax treatments to reduce the overall tax burden.

1. **Income Tax Strategies**: Optimizing income through salary, dividends, and bonuses in a manner that aligns with current tax brackets can significantly reduce tax liabilities. Advanced strategies may include deferring income or accelerating expenses to manage taxable income levels.

2. **Capital Gains Tax Planning**: For businesses with appreciating assets, planning around capital gains tax—including timing of asset sales and leveraging the step-up in basis for inherited assets—can result in substantial tax savings.

3. **Estate and Gift Tax Planning**: Understanding the implications of transferring business ownership, either during the owner's lifetime or as part of an estate, can influence the timing and method of transfers to minimize estate and gift taxes.

Utilizing Business Structures and Agreements

The choice of business structure—sole proprietorship, partnership, LLC, S Corporation, or C Corporation—plays a significant role in tax planning. Each structure has distinct tax implications, affecting how profits are taxed and the owner's personal liability.

- **LLCs and S Corporations** often offer favorable pass-through taxation, allowing business income to be taxed at personal income tax rates, potentially avoiding double taxation.
- **C Corporations** are subject to corporate income tax, but careful planning around dividends and retained earnings can mitigate the impact of double taxation.

Buy-sell agreements and shareholder agreements are also vital, outlining how ownership transitions will occur and the tax implications of these transitions.

Retirement Planning and Tax Benefits

Integrating retirement planning into the tax strategy allows business owners to reduce taxable income through contributions to retirement accounts, such as 401(k)s or SEP IRAs. These contributions not only provide a tax benefit but also secure the owner's financial future.

Advanced Tax Planning Techniques

- **Charitable Contributions**: Utilizing charitable giving, including donating appreciated assets or setting up charitable trusts, can offer tax deductions and reduce taxable estate size.
- **Asset Location**: Strategically locating investments across taxable and tax-advantaged accounts can optimize the tax efficiency of investment income and gains.
- **Tax Loss Harvesting**: This involves selling securities at a loss to offset capital gains tax liabilities, a strategy that requires careful timing and management.
- **Life Insurance Policies**: Properly structured life insurance can provide liquidity for estate taxes and other obligations, ensuring the business can continue without needing to liquidate assets.

Keeping Abreast of Tax Law Changes

Tax laws are constantly evolving, making it essential for business owners to stay informed about changes that could impact their business and personal finances. Regular reviews of the tax plan, in consultation with tax professionals, ensure strategies remain aligned with current laws and the owner's goals.

Liability Protection and Asset Separation

For business owners, protecting personal assets from business liabilities is a fundamental aspect of financial planning and risk management. This concept, known as asset separation, is crucial in safeguarding an owner's personal estate from the potential fallout of business debts, lawsuits, or other financial obligations. Implementing strategies for liability protection and asset separation not only secures the owner's personal financial future but also ensures that the business can weather legal and financial storms.

Understanding Liability in Business Structures

The choice of a business structure has profound implications for liability and asset protection. This decision can determine the extent to which a business owner's personal assets are at risk in the face of business debts or legal actions. Let's delve into the nuances of different business structures, focusing on sole proprietorships, partnerships, limited liability companies (LLCs), and corporations, with real-world examples to illustrate these concepts.

Sole Proprietorships and Partnerships

In sole proprietorships and partnerships, the business and the owner are legally considered the same entity. This means there is no legal shield separating the owner's personal assets from the business's liabilities. If the business incurs debt or faces a lawsuit, personal assets like the owner's home, car, and savings can be at risk.

- **Example**: Consider Jane, who runs a local bakery as a sole proprietor. When a customer falls ill alleging food poisoning from the bakery and sues for damages, Jane's personal assets could be used to cover any legal settlements or debts arising from the lawsuit, potentially devastating her personal financial security.

Limited Liability Companies (LLCs)

LLCs offer a legal separation between personal assets and business liabilities. This structure creates a protective veil, often referred to as the "corporate veil," which shields owners' (members') personal assets from being used to satisfy business debts or judgments.

- **Example**: Alex owns a consulting firm structured as an LLC. When the firm faces a lawsuit from a disgruntled client, only the assets within the LLC can be targeted for any potential legal settlements. Alex's personal assets, such as his home and personal savings, are protected from being claimed to settle business debts.

Corporations (C-Corps and S-Corps)

Corporations, whether C-Corps or S-Corps, offer the strongest level of personal liability protection. As entities completely separate from their owners (shareholders), corporations bear their own legal responsibilities. Shareholders' personal assets are generally safe from corporate liabilities and legal actions against the corporation.

- **Example**: Sara and Tom operate a manufacturing company structured as a corporation. Despite facing a significant product liability claim, their personal assets remain untouched by the lawsuit. The corporate structure ensures that only the assets owned by the corporation can be used to address any legal liabilities.

Considerations for Choosing a Business Structure

Choosing between these structures involves balancing the desire for liability protection with other factors, such as tax implications, operational flexibility, and administrative requirements. While LLCs and corporations offer substantial liability protection, they come with more complex regulations and potential tax burdens. Sole proprietorships and partnerships offer simplicity and tax benefits but lack in terms of personal asset protection.

The Importance of Proper Structuring and Formalities

Even with LLCs and corporations, maintaining the separation of personal and business assets requires adherence to certain formalities:

- **Maintaining Separate Finances**: Business and personal finances should not be commingled. Separate bank accounts and financial records are essential.

- **Adhering to Legal Requirements**: Corporations and LLCs must follow state-specific legal requirements, including filing annual reports, holding meetings, and keeping records, to preserve the liability shield.

Strategies for Asset Protection

1. **Choose the Right Business Entity**: Opting for an LLC or corporation can provide significant protection for personal assets. These entities treat the business as a separate legal individual, limiting the owner's liability to their investment in the business.

2. **Maintain Corporate Formalities**: For LLCs and corporations, it's vital to follow all legal requirements, such as holding regular meetings, keeping minutes, and maintaining separate financial accounts, to ensure the entity's liability protection isn't compromised.

3. **Use Insurance as a Safety Net**: Comprehensive business insurance, including general liability, professional liability, and product liability insurance, can provide an added layer of protection against claims and lawsuits.

4. **Employ Estate Planning Tools**: Trusts can be an effective way to protect personal assets. Assets owned by an irrevocable trust are generally considered separate from the business owner's personal estate, offering protection from business liabilities.

5. **Separate Personal and Business Finances**: Keeping personal and business finances distinct is critical. This includes having separate bank accounts, credit cards, and financial records. Commingling funds can jeopardize the legal separation between personal and business assets.

6. **Asset Ownership Strategies**: Owning personal assets, like your home or investments, jointly with a spouse or in a trust can offer additional layers of protection from creditors.

Strategies for Asset Protection

1. **Choose the Right Business Entity**: Opting for an LLC or corporation can provide significant protection for personal assets. These entities treat the business as a separate legal individual, limiting the owner's liability to their investment in the business.

2. **Maintain Corporate Formalities**: For LLCs and corporations, it's vital to follow all legal requirements, such as holding regular meetings, keeping minutes, and maintaining separate financial accounts, to ensure the entity's liability protection isn't compromised.

3. **Use Insurance as a Safety Net**: Comprehensive business insurance, including general liability, professional liability, and product liability insurance, can offer an added layer of protection against claims and lawsuits.

4. **Employ Estate Planning Tools**: Trusts can be an effective way to protect personal assets. Assets owned by an irrevocable trust are generally considered separate from the business owner's personal estate, offering protection from business liabilities.

5. **Separate Personal and Business Finances**: Keeping personal and business finances distinct is critical. This includes having separate bank accounts, credit cards, and financial records. Commingling funds can jeopardize the legal separation between personal and business assets.

6. **Asset Ownership Strategies**: Owning personal assets, like your home or investments, jointly with a spouse or in a trust can offer additional layers of protection from creditors.

PART IV: THE ROLE OF LIFE INSURANCE IN SIMPLE ESTATE PLANNING

Life insurance is more than just a way to provide money for your family after you're gone. While it's commonly seen as a basic part of planning for the future, it actually plays a much bigger role in what's called estate planning. Estate planning is how you organize your finances and assets to make sure they're handled the way you want after you pass away. Life insurance is a key part of this because it can do a lot more than just give your family money; it can be a strategic tool to protect your financial legacy and make sure your wealth is passed on smoothly from one generation to the next.

At its core, life insurance is simple: you pay for a policy, and when you die, the insurance company pays a set amount of money to the people you choose, called beneficiaries. This helps make sure they're financially okay if you're not around. But when you start planning your estate—figuring out how to manage and pass on everything you own—life insurance shows how versatile it really is. It can help manage estate taxes (the taxes that can come when transferring wealth after someone dies), provide cash when it's needed, help keep a family business running, and ensure all your children receive an equal share of your wealth, even if not all assets are easily divided.

Using life insurance in estate planning isn't just for the super-rich who are worried about big estate taxes. It's something anyone thinking about how to leave their assets can use. It offers a way to solve common issues many families face, like covering expenses right after death, keeping a business within the family, or supporting charitable causes you care about. Life insurance is a crucial piece in these plans, helping achieve your goals and taking care of your loved ones exactly how you intend.

In simpler terms, life insurance in estate planning lets you use the money from your policy in smart ways to ensure your family and your wishes are taken care of after you're gone. Whether you're just starting to think about how to leave your assets or looking to add to your existing plans, understanding how to use life insurance effectively can make a big difference in protecting your legacy and ensuring your wishes are followed.

Understanding the Basics of Life Insurance

At its core, life insurance is a contract between you and an insurance company. You agree to pay regular amounts of money (premiums) to the company, and in exchange, the company promises to pay a lump sum (death benefit) to your beneficiaries after you pass away. This money can help cover living expenses, debts, or any specific financial needs your family might have, ensuring they're taken care of financially when you're not around.

Types of Life Insurance

There are two main types of life insurance policies to consider: term life insurance and permanent life insurance. Each has its unique features and benefits.

1. **Term Life Insurance**: This type is like renting an insurance policy for a specific period, usually 10, 20, or 30 years. If you pass away during this term, your beneficiaries receive the death benefit. It's generally less expensive than permanent life insurance but doesn't accumulate any cash value. It's a good choice if you're looking for coverage during your working years or while paying off a mortgage.

2. **Permanent Life Insurance**: This type covers you for your entire life, as long as you keep paying the premiums. It's more expensive than term life because it also acts as a financial tool, accumulating cash value over time that you can borrow against if needed. There are several kinds of permanent life insurance, including:

   - **Whole Life Insurance**: Offers a fixed premium and death benefit with a cash value that grows at a guaranteed rate.
   - **Universal Life Insurance**: Provides more flexibility in premiums, death benefits, and savings elements, allowing you to adjust your policy as your financial needs change.
   - **Variable Life Insurance**: Allows you to invest the policy's cash value in various accounts for potentially higher growth, though it comes with more risk.

Choosing the Right Life Insurance Policy

Selecting the appropriate life insurance policy is a pivotal decision in financial planning, impacting your estate's liquidity, tax implications, and the financial well-being of your beneficiaries. With a myriad of options available, understanding the nuances of each type of policy and aligning them with your estate planning goals is crucial. The next pages aim to explore the considerations for choosing the right life insurance policy, focusing on the individual's needs, the benefits of different policies, and how they fit into a comprehensive estate plan.

Assessing Your Needs

The first step in choosing the right life insurance policy is a thorough assessment of your financial situation and long-term objectives:

- **Financial Obligations**: Consider debts, mortgages, and other financial responsibilities that would need to be covered in your absence.

- **Income Replacement**: Estimate the amount your family would need to maintain their standard of living without your income.
- **Future Financial Goals**: Factor in future expenses like college tuition for children or a spouse's retirement needs.

Understanding Policy Types

With your financial needs in mind, compare the characteristics of term and permanent life insurance policies to determine which aligns with your estate planning goals:

1. **Term Life Insurance**: Suitable for those seeking affordable, straightforward coverage for a specific period. It's ideal if your primary concern is providing financial security during your working years or covering a mortgage.

   Pros: Lower premiums, simple to understand.

   Cons: No cash value accumulation, coverage ends after the term unless renewed.

2. **Permanent Life Insurance**: Offers lifelong coverage and includes a cash value component, appealing to those interested in wealth accumulation and estate planning flexibility.

- **Whole Life Insurance**:

  Pros: Fixed premiums, guaranteed death benefit, and cash value growth.

  Cons: Higher premiums compared to term life.

- **Universal Life Insurance**:

  Pros: Flexible premiums and death benefits, potential for higher cash value growth.

  Cons: More complex, with varying costs and potential for decreased cash value if not managed carefully.

- **Variable Life Insurance**:

  Pros: Investment options for cash value, potential for high returns.

  Cons: Higher risk and costs, cash value can fluctuate based on investment performance.

Integrating Life Insurance into Estate Planning

- **Trust Ownership**: Consider establishing an irrevocable life insurance trust (ILIT), which we'll discuss later, to own the policy, which can keep the proceeds out of your taxable estate, providing both liquidity for estate taxes and ensuring that the death benefit directly supports your estate planning objectives without increasing tax liabilities.
- **Beneficiary Considerations**: Align beneficiary designations with your overall estate plan to ensure seamless asset distribution. Regularly review these designations to reflect changes in your family dynamics or estate planning goals.

Evaluating Cost vs. Benefit

Assess the cost of premiums in relation to your budget and financial goals. While term life insurance offers lower premiums, permanent life insurance provides added benefits like cash value growth and estate planning flexibility. Weigh these costs against the potential long-term benefits for your estate and beneficiaries.

Seeking Professional Advice

Given the complexity of choosing the right life insurance policy and integrating it into your estate plan, consulting with financial advisors and estate planning professionals is advisable. They can offer personalized advice based on your financial situation, estate planning goals, and the latest tax implications.

Strategic Benefits of Life Insurance in Estate Planning

Life insurance plays a crucial role in estate planning, offering a suite of strategic benefits that extend beyond providing a financial safety net for beneficiaries. Its versatility makes it an invaluable tool for addressing various estate planning challenges, including liquidity needs, tax planning, and wealth transfer strategies. This section explores the multifaceted advantages of incorporating life insurance into your estate plan.

Liquidity for Estate Settlement

One of the most immediate benefits of life insurance is its ability to provide liquidity at a critical time. Estate settlement can incur various expenses, from funeral costs to outstanding debts and taxes, which might necessitate the liquidation of assets under less-than-ideal market conditions.

- **Immediate Access to Funds**: Life insurance proceeds are typically available soon after the policyholder's death, offering a timely source of funds to cover these expenses without the need to sell other estate assets.
- **Bypassing Probate**: Policies with named beneficiaries can bypass the probate process, ensuring that funds are directly available to beneficiaries without delay.

Managing Estate Taxes

For larger estates potentially subject to estate taxes, life insurance serves as a strategic tool for managing these liabilities.

- The death benefit from a life insurance policy can be used to pay estate taxes, preserving the value of the estate for the heirs.
- **Irrevocable Life Insurance Trust (ILIT)**: By placing a life insurance policy in an ILIT, the proceeds from the policy can be excluded from the taxable estate, potentially saving significant amounts in estate taxes. We'll discuss this in the next chapter.

Equalizing Inheritances

Life insurance offers a solution for equalizing inheritances among heirs, particularly in situations where the estate comprises assets that cannot be easily divided, such as a family business.

- **Providing Equivalent Value**: Policyholders can use life insurance proceeds to provide equivalent inheritances to heirs who might not be involved in a family business or who prefer cash to physical assets.
- **Minimizing Conflict**: This strategy can help minimize potential conflicts among heirs by ensuring a fair distribution of the estate's value.

Business Succession Planning

For business owners, life insurance is a key component of succession planning, ensuring the continuity of the business and providing for a smooth transition of ownership.

- **Buy-Sell Agreements**

  A buy-sell agreement is a legally binding arrangement between business partners that outlines how a partner's share of the business will be reassigned if they die, become incapacitated, or leave the company. Life insurance policies are commonly used to fund these agreements, providing the necessary funds to purchase the departing partner's interest.

  Imagine a scenario where three individuals co-own a technology firm. They enter into a buy-sell agreement funded by life insurance policies on each partner. If one partner unexpectedly passes away, the life insurance policy pays out a death benefit to the surviving partners. This payout is then used to buy the deceased partner's shares from their estate at a previously agreed-upon price. As a result, the business can continue operating without financial strain, and the deceased partner's beneficiaries are compensated fairly and promptly.

- **Key Person Insurance**

  Key person insurance is a life insurance policy taken out by the business on the lives of individuals whose knowledge, work, or overall contribution is considered uniquely valuable to the company. The business pays the premiums and is also the beneficiary of the policy. This insurance provides a financial cushion that can help cover the costs of finding and training a replacement, compensating for lost sales, or even facilitating a business closure if necessary. Consider a small winery with a winemaker whose expertise significantly contributes to the business's success. The winery purchases a key person insurance policy on the winemaker. If the winemaker were to pass away unexpectedly, the winery would receive the insurance payout. This financial influx could be used to cover the search for a skilled successor, mitigate any immediate financial losses due to the winemaker's absence, and ensure the business maintains its operational stability during the transition.

Both buy-sell agreements and key person insurance mitigate risks associated with the sudden loss of a business owner or essential employee. They ensure that the business can continue to thrive or transition smoothly without causing undue financial strain on the company or the deceased's family.

The strategic incorporation of life insurance into estate planning offers a range of benefits, from providing essential liquidity and managing estate taxes to equalizing inheritances among heirs and facilitating business succession. By carefully selecting and structuring life insurance policies, individuals can address specific estate planning challenges, ensuring their legacy is preserved and their estate is passed on according to their wishes.

Advanced Strategies: Irrevocable Life Insurance Trusts (ILITs)

In the sophisticated landscape of estate planning, Irrevocable Life Insurance Trusts (ILITs) represent a powerful strategy for managing estate taxes and preserving wealth for future generations. By removing life insurance proceeds from your taxable estate, ILITs can significantly reduce estate tax liabilities while providing financial benefits to your beneficiaries.

How ILITs Work

An ILIT, once established, cannot be altered or revoked. The ILIT becomes the owner and beneficiary of one or more life insurance policies. When the grantor (the person who establishes the trust) passes away, the death benefit from the insurance policies is paid directly to the ILIT, bypassing the grantor's estate and thus not being subject to estate taxes.

Here's an examination of how ILITs function, from setup to execution, emphasizing the practicalities and implications for estate planning.

Establishing an ILIT

1. **Creation of the Trust**: The process begins with the drafting of the trust document by an estate planning attorney. This document outlines the terms, including the trustee's appointment, the beneficiaries, and how the trust proceeds should be managed and distributed.

2. **Transferring Ownership of Life Insurance Policies**: The next step involves transferring the ownership of an existing life insurance policy to the ILIT or having the ILIT purchase a new policy directly. This transfer is crucial as it removes the policy's proceeds from the grantor's taxable estate.

3. **Funding the ILIT**: The grantor makes cash gifts to the ILIT, which the trustee then uses to pay the life insurance premiums. These gifts often qualify for the annual gift tax exclusion, reducing the grantor's taxable estate further.

4. **Trustee's Role**: The trustee administers the ILIT according to the trust document's terms, managing the life insurance policy(ies), paying premiums, and ultimately distributing the death benefits to the beneficiaries as instructed.

Let's walk through a hypothetical scenario to illustrate the process of establishing an ILIT, featuring a character named Sophia, a successful entrepreneur with a growing estate concerned about estate taxes and providing for her family.

Step 1: Decision to Create an ILIT

Sophia consults with her estate planning attorney, expressing her desire to ensure her estate passes efficiently to her children while minimizing estate taxes. After reviewing her options, Sophia decides to establish an ILIT as part of her comprehensive estate plan. She chooses her long-time friend, Marcus, as the trustee due to his financial savvy and trustworthiness.

Step 2: Drafting the Trust Document

Sophia's attorney drafts the ILIT document, specifying:

The trust's purpose: To own a life insurance policy on Sophia's life and to distribute the proceeds to her children, Liam and Emma, upon her death.

Marcus's duties as the trustee, including paying life insurance premiums and managing the distribution of death benefits.

Distribution terms: The proceeds are to be held in trust for Liam and Emma until they reach the age of 30, with allowances for their education and healthcare before this age.

Step 3: Funding the ILIT and Purchasing Life Insurance

million life insurance policy on Sophia's life, naming the ILIT as both the owner and beneficiary of the policy. To comply with the IRS's three-year rule, which states that if the insured dies within three years of transferring ownership of a life insurance policy to another party, the policy proceeds will be included in their estate for estate tax purposes, the policy is purchased directly by the ILIT, avoiding this potential complication.

Step 4: Annual Gifts to Fund Premiums

Sophia decides to fund the life insurance premiums through annual gifts to the ILIT. She utilizes the annual gift tax exclusion ($18,000 per recipient in 2024) to make these gifts tax-efficient. Since the ILIT benefits both Liam and Emma, she can gift $30,000 total per year without exceeding the exclusion limit. Marcus, as the trustee, sends out Crummey (I will explain this term at the end of the chapter) letters to Liam and Emma each year, notifying them of their right to withdraw a portion of the gifted funds for a limited period, a requirement for the gifts to qualify for the annual gift tax exclusion.

Step 5: Managing the ILIT

Over the years, Marcus faithfully manages the ILIT, paying the insurance premiums and investing the remaining funds according to the trust's terms. He keeps detailed records of all transactions and communicates regularly with Sophia about the trust's status.

Step 6: Distribution Upon Sophia's Death

Many years later, when Sophia passes away, the $3 million life insurance policy pays out to the ILIT, free from Sophia's taxable estate. Marcus then manages the distribution according to the ILIT's terms. Since both Liam and Emma are over 30, he distributes the proceeds to them outright, providing a significant financial benefit that is not subject to estate taxes. Had they been under 30, the funds would have been held in trust, with distributions made for their education and healthcare as per the ILIT's instructions.

This practical example illustrates how an ILIT can be effectively established and utilized to provide a tax-efficient means of transferring wealth to beneficiaries while ensuring that the life insurance proceeds are protected from estate taxes and managed according to the grantor's wishes. Sophia's foresight in creating the ILIT, coupled with Marcus's diligent management, ensures that her estate planning goals are achieved, providing significant financial support to her children without the burden of estate taxes.

Mechanisms for Beneficiary Distribution

Upon the death of the grantor, the life insurance policy within the ILIT pays out the death benefit directly to the trust. This payout is not included in the grantor's estate, thus not subject to estate taxes. The trustee then distributes the proceeds to the beneficiaries according to the grantor's outlined wishes. These distributions can be:

- **Immediate and Lump-Sum**: Beneficiaries receive their share of the trust assets all at once.
- **Staggered Over Time**: Beneficiaries receive distributions at specific ages or milestones, providing ongoing financial support.
- **For Specific Purposes**: Distributions may be designated for particular uses, like education expenses or healthcare needs, offering targeted financial support.

Crummey Explained:

"Crummey" withdrawal rights are a special rule used when giving money to a type of trust called an Irrevocable Life Insurance Trust (ILIT), which owns a life insurance policy. This rule is named after a legal case that made it clear these rights are allowed. When someone puts money into this trust to pay for the insurance policy, it's like giving a gift to the people who will benefit from the trust, like family members. To not have to pay gift taxes on this money (up to $18,000 per person each year), there's a catch: the gift has to be something the beneficiary can use right away.

But here's the tricky part: the money given to the trust doesn't go directly to the beneficiaries because it's used to pay for the life insurance policy instead. So, to make sure these gifts still count for the tax break, the trust gives the beneficiaries a chance to take out some of the money for a short time after each contribution is made. This opportunity is told to beneficiaries through something called a "Crummey letter."

Here's how it works in simpler terms:

1. **Notification**: Right after the trust gets a money gift, it sends out these "Crummey letters" to let the beneficiaries know they can take out their part of the money if they want to, but only for about 30 days.

2. **Temporary Chance to Use the Gift**: If the beneficiaries decide they want to use their chance to take out the money, they can. This makes the money a "present interest" gift because they could use it right away. If they don't take the money out, it stays in the trust to help pay for the insurance.

3. **No Extra Taxes**: Because the beneficiaries had a real chance to get the money right away, the IRS says, "Okay, this counts as a gift that doesn't need extra taxes." This means the person who put the money into the trust can give up to $18,000 per beneficiary each year without it counting against their big lifetime limit for giving gifts or causing any gift taxes.

"Crummey" rights are a clever way to make sure money given to this special trust counts as a gift that gets a tax break, even though the money is really going to pay for life insurance. It's a bit like saying, "Hey, you can have this money now if you really want it," knowing it will help in the long run if they leave it to pay the insurance. This helps everyone involved save on taxes and make the most of the trust and life insurance policy.

Tax Implications and Advantages of ILITs

Estate Tax Implications

Exclusion from the Taxable Estate: When a life insurance policy is owned by an individual, the death benefit is included in the policyholder's taxable estate, potentially subjecting it to high estate taxes. However, an ILIT, as the policy owner, removes the death benefit from the grantor's estate. This means that when the insured (grantor) passes away, the life insurance proceeds paid to the ILIT do not increase the value of the estate for estate tax purposes.

Example: If a policyholder owns a $2 million life insurance policy at death, and the estate tax exemption is $11.7 million, the policy proceeds might push the total estate value over the exemption limit, resulting in estate taxes. By using an ILIT, these proceeds are not counted towards the estate value, potentially saving hundreds of thousands in taxes.

Gift Tax Implications

Annual Contributions and Gift Taxes: The grantor makes annual gifts to the ILIT to fund the life insurance premiums. These gifts can qualify for the annual gift tax exclusion ($18,000 per recipient in 2024), allowing the grantor to fund the policy without incurring gift taxes. This is contingent on the ILIT providing beneficiaries with "Crummey" withdrawal rights, which give them the temporary right to withdraw contributions, thereby qualifying the gifts for the annual exclusion.

Example: Suppose a grantor contributes $30,000 annually to an ILIT to cover premiums, and the ILIT has two beneficiaries. The grantor can use the annual gift tax exclusion to make these gifts tax-free, reducing their taxable estate each year by $30,000 without eating into their lifetime gift and estate tax exemption amount.

Generation-Skipping Transfer (GST) Tax Implications

Protecting Multiple Generations: ILITs can be designed to benefit not just the grantor's immediate children but also successive generations. By doing so, ILITs can help avoid or minimize GST taxes that apply to transfers to grandchildren and beyond if the transfers exceed the GST tax exemption limit.

Strategic Planning: Proper structuring of an ILIT can allocate the grantor's GST tax exemption to the trust, ensuring that the life insurance proceeds benefit multiple generations without incurring additional GST taxes.

Liquidity and Estate Taxes

ILITs provide liquidity to estates for paying estate taxes and other costs without needing to sell other estate assets. This liquidity is especially beneficial for estates composed largely of illiquid assets like real estate or closely held businesses.

Navigating Legal and Financial Considerations

Integrating life insurance into your estate plan involves facing a series of legal and financial considerations to ensure that your strategy aligns with your overall objectives. This integration is crucial for maximizing the benefits of life insurance, including tax advantages, asset protection, and providing for your beneficiaries in the most effective way possible. Here's a guide to understanding and managing these considerations.

Aligning Life Insurance with Estate Goals

1. **Clarify Your Estate Planning Objectives**: Begin by identifying what you aim to achieve with your estate plan. Whether it's providing financial security for your family, supporting

charitable causes, or ensuring the continuity of a family business, your goals will dictate how best to use life insurance within your estate plan.

2. **Assess Your Financial Landscape**: Take a comprehensive look at your financial situation, including your assets, liabilities, and potential estate tax exposure. This assessment will help you determine the type and amount of life insurance coverage needed to address potential gaps or liabilities.

Legal Structures and Ownership

1. **Policy Ownership**: Deciding who should own the life insurance policy (the insured individual, a trust, or another entity) is a critical legal consideration. Ownership affects the policy's inclusion in your taxable estate and can have significant tax implications.

2. **Use of Trusts**: For many, placing a life insurance policy in a trust, such as an ILIT, offers considerable benefits, including keeping the policy proceeds out of the taxable estate. However, this requires careful planning to ensure the trust is properly structured and administered according to both state laws and your estate planning goals.

3. **Beneficiary Designations**: Ensure that the beneficiary designations on your life insurance policy are consistent with your overall estate plan. Incorrect or outdated designations can lead to unintended consequences and may undermine your estate planning objectives.

Financial Considerations

1. **Funding Strategies**: Explore various funding strategies for your life insurance policy, considering premium costs and how they fit within your overall financial plan. This might involve annual gifting strategies within the limits of the gift tax exclusion, particularly if using an ILIT.

2. **Tax Implications**: Understand the potential tax implications of your life insurance policy including income, estate, and gift taxes. Proper planning can help minimize tax liabilities and maximize the value passed on to your beneficiaries.

Coordination with Other Estate Planning Instruments

Integrating life insurance into your estate plan is not an isolated task; it requires careful coordination with other estate planning instruments to ensure a seamless, effective strategy. This coordination is vital to prevent overlaps, gaps, and contradictions within your estate plan, guaranteeing that all components work in tandem to fulfill your estate planning objectives. Here's a look at how life insurance can be harmonized with other key estate planning tools.

While a will dictates the distribution of your assets upon your death, life insurance provides immediate financial support to your beneficiaries. Ensure that your will and the beneficiary designations on your life insurance policy do not conflict but rather complement each other. For example, if certain assets are intended for specific heirs as outlined in your will, your life insurance proceeds can be allocated to different needs or beneficiaries, filling any financial gaps.

Naming a trust as the beneficiary of your life insurance policy can streamline the management and distribution of the death benefit. This approach is particularly useful when you wish to provide for minors, manage the inheritance for spendthrift beneficiaries, or when you're aiming for specific tax advantages, as with an ILIT. The trust document should clearly outline how the proceeds from the life insurance policy are to be used, ensuring alignment with your broader estate objectives.

Powers of Attorney and Health Care Directives

While life insurance addresses the financial aspects of your estate plan, powers of attorney (POA) and health care directives cover decision-making in the event of incapacitation. It's crucial to ensure that the individuals you've designated as your POA or health care proxy are aware of your life insurance policies and your intentions for their proceeds. This awareness can help in making informed decisions about your health care and financial management, especially in critical situations.

Business Succession Plans

For business owners, integrating life insurance into business succession plans is essential. Buy-sell agreements funded through life insurance give a clear path for business continuity and can prevent potential disputes among surviving partners or family members. Ensure that the terms of the buy-sell agreement and the ownership and beneficiary designations of the life insurance policy are consistent and support the agreed-upon business succession strategy.

Charitable Giving Plans

If charitable giving is a component of your estate plan, life insurance can serve as a means to fulfill your philanthropic goals. Designating a charity as a beneficiary of a life insurance policy can ensure a significant gift to the organization upon your death. Coordination is necessary to ensure that this charitable intent is reflected across your estate planning documents, providing clarity and preventing any unintended use of the assets.

Professional Coordination

Given the complexities involved in aligning life insurance with other estate planning instruments, engaging with a team of professionals—estate planning attorneys, financial advisors, and tax experts—is recommended. These professionals can help:

Review and Align Documents: Ensure that all estate planning documents are up-to-date and reflect your current wishes, with no discrepancies among beneficiary designations, wills, trusts, and other planning tools.

Strategize for Tax Efficiency: Offer guidance on structuring your estate plan, including life insurance, for maximum tax efficiency and asset protection.

Customize Solutions: Tailor estate planning strategies to your unique situation, considering family dynamics, business interests, philanthropic goals, and financial circumstances.

CONCLUSION

As we close the final pages of this comprehensive guide to estate planning, it's my hope that you now stand equipped with the knowledge, strategies, and confidence to navigate the future of your estate. The journey doesn't end here; it evolves with your life's milestones, ensuring that your legacy is preserved and your loved ones are cared for according to your wishes.

Throughout this book, we've ventured through the essential concepts of estate planning, from the foundations laid out in Part I to the complex tax strategies unveiled in Part III. We've examined the tools at your disposal, such as wills, trusts, and powers of attorney, and outlined the critical role life insurance can play in securing your financial legacy.

You've learned not only how to articulate your wishes but also how to safeguard your assets, minimize your tax liabilities, and avoid the potential pitfalls that can arise without proper planning. The real-life stories and legal explanations were provided to clarify the significance of each step in this crucial process.

As you implement the strategies discussed, remember that estate planning is an ongoing process that should adapt to the changing landscapes of your life and the legal world. Regular reviews and adjustments are essential to ensure that your plan remains effective and reflective of your current situation and future goals.

If this book has helped you gain clarity and direction in preparing your estate plan, I would be grateful if you took a moment to leave a review by scanning the QR Code below. Your insights could guide others to find the same confidence and peace of mind that comes with well-structured estate planning.

For those who have journeyed with me from the beginning to this point, I extend my deepest thanks. It has been an honor to share this guidance with you. Should you wish to delve deeper into the subject or seek additional resources, remember to access the exclusive bonus material available to you.

As you move forward, may you do so with the assurance that you have taken the necessary steps to protect and honor your legacy. Estate planning is one of the most profound acts of foresight and care one can undertake—it is your final gift to those you cherish most.

GLOSSARY

Ancillary Probate: A supplementary probate process required for assets located in different jurisdictions from where the primary probate is conducted.

Annual Gift Tax Exclusion: The amount an individual can gift to another individual without incurring gift taxes, set at $18,000 per recipient for 2024.

Asset Distribution: The allocation of an individual's estate to their chosen beneficiaries through a will, trust, or as dictated by law if there is no will.

Asset Protection: Legal strategies to protect assets from creditors, lawsuits, or judgments, often involving trusts.

Asset Separation: The practice of keeping personal assets distinct from business assets to protect them from business liabilities.

Asset Valuation: The process of determining the fair market value of assets, essential for various aspects of estate planning, including equitable distribution and tax planning.

Beneficiaries: Individuals or entities designated to receive the death benefit from a life insurance policy.

Beneficiary Designations: A financial account designation that allows the account's proceeds to bypass the probate process and go directly to the named beneficiaries upon the account holder's death.

Bequest: The act of giving or leaving personal property by a will.

Business Continuity: The aspect of estate planning that ensures the seamless transition of a business after the owner's death.

Business Structure: The legal form of a business, such as sole proprietorship, partnership, LLC, or corporation, each with unique implications for estate planning, especially regarding liability and tax treatment.

Business Valuation: The process of determining the economic value of a business, critical for estate tax calculations, succession planning, and asset distribution.

Buy-Sell Agreement: A legally binding agreement outlining how a partner's share of a business will be reallocated if they die or leave the company, often funded by life insurance.

Capital Gains Tax: A tax on the profit from the sale of non-inventory assets, such as stocks or property, when the sale price exceeds the purchase price.

Cash Value: A savings component of permanent life insurance that accumulates tax-deferred over the life of the policy.

Charitable Contributions: Donations left to charitable organizations as part of one's estate, which can also provide tax benefits.

Charitable Giving: The act of donating to charitable organizations, which can be structured through trusts for tax benefits.

Charitable Lead Trusts (CLTs): An irrevocable trust that donates income to charity first, with the remainder going to non-charitable beneficiaries, potentially offering gift or estate tax deductions.

Charitable Remainder Trusts (CRTs): An irrevocable trust that provides income to non-charitable beneficiaries with the remainder going to charity, offering immediate tax deductions and reducing estate taxes.

Charitable Trust: A trust set up to benefit a charitable organization or the public good, offering estate tax benefits.

Codicil: An addition or supplement that explains, modifies, or revokes a will or part of one.

Corporate Veil: The legal concept separating the actions and liabilities of a corporation from its shareholders, providing protection for personal assets.

Crummey Letter: A notice given to beneficiaries of an ILIT, allowing them the temporary right to withdraw contributions to qualify gifts for the annual gift tax exclusion.

Death Benefit: The money paid to beneficiaries upon the insured's death, providing financial support and contributing to the estate's liquidity.

Digital Assets: Online properties and accounts, including cryptocurrencies, social media profiles, and digital copyrights.

Donor-Advised Funds (DAFs): Philanthropic funds that allow donors to make charitable contributions, receive immediate tax deductions, and recommend grants to charities over time.

Durable Power of Attorney: Remains effective even if the principal becomes incapacitated.

Equitable Distribution: The fair and just division of property between spouses upon divorce or, in estate planning, among heirs according to the decedent's wishes.

Estate Liquidity: The availability of cash or assets easily convertible to cash to pay estate taxes, debts, and other expenses upon death.

Estate Planning Instruments: Legal tools such as wills, trusts, POAs, and healthcare directives used to ensure an individual's wishes are carried out after death.

Estate Planning: The process of arranging the management and disposal of a person's estate during their life and after death, involving the creation of documents to outline the distribution of assets and care for dependents.

Estate Settlement Costs: Expenses associated with administering an estate after death, including funeral expenses, debts, and taxes, which life insurance proceeds can help cover.

Estate Tax: A tax on the right to transfer property upon death, applicable to estate values above a certain threshold.

Estate: The total sum of an individual's assets and liabilities, including tangible and intangible items such as real estate, vehicles, bank accounts, stocks, and personal belongings.

Executor: The appointed individual responsible for carrying out the instructions in a will, managing the estate's settlement through probate.

Federal Estate Taxes: Taxes imposed by the federal government on estates exceeding a certain exemption threshold, which is adjusted periodically.

Fiduciary: An entity or person with a legal obligation to act in the best interest of another party, such as a trustee or executor.

Financial Legacy: The financial assets and estate left behind by an individual after death, which life insurance can help protect and preserve for future generations.

Financial Power of Attorney: A legal document that grants an individual the authority to act on another's behalf in financial matters.

Form 1041: The U.S. Income Tax Return for Estates and Trusts, required if the estate generates more than $600 in annual gross income.

Funding the Trust: The process of transferring ownership of assets into a trust.

General Power of Attorney: Grants broad powers to manage a wide range of financial and legal matters.

Gift Taxes: A tax on the transfer of property by one individual to another while receiving nothing or less than full value in return.

Gifts: Transfers of assets made during the grantor's lifetime, potentially reducing estate taxes and providing immediate benefits to the recipients.

Grantor Trusts: Trusts that are irrevocable, where the income generated is taxed to the grantor not the trust, which can provide income tax benefits and reduce estate taxes.

Grantor/Settlor/Trustor: The individual who creates a trust and transfers ownership of asset into it.

Guardianship: A legal status where an individual is appointed to care for a minor child and their property in the event of the parents' incapacity or death.

Health Care Directives: Instructions for medical care preferences and appointment of a health care decision-maker if one becomes incapacitated.

Healthcare Power of Attorney: A legal document that designates an individual to make medical decisions for someone else if they become incapacitated.

Holographic Will: A will entirely written, dated, and signed in the handwriting of the person making it.

Income in Respect of a Decedent (IRD): Income that the deceased was entitled to but did not receive before their death, which is subject to income tax when received by the estate or beneficiaries.

Income Taxes: Taxes on the income generated by the deceased's estate after their death, which may include income from interest, dividends, or property rentals.

Inheritance Taxes: State-level taxes imposed on the beneficiaries receiving assets from an estate, varying in rates depending on the beneficiary's relationship to the deceased.

Insurance Policies: Financial products that can protect business owners from specific risks and provide liquidity for estate obligations.

Intangible Assets: Non-physical assets including financial accounts, stocks, bonds, and intellectual property.

Intestacy: The condition of dying without a will or having a will that only covers part of the estate, resulting in the distribution of assets according to state laws.

Intestate: The condition of dying without a valid will, resulting in state laws determining the estate's distribution.

Inventory of Assets: A comprehensive list detailing all assets owned by an individual, including real estate, bank accounts, investments, and personal property.

Irrevocable Life Insurance Trust (ILIT): A trust designed to exclude life insurance proceeds from the insured's estate, reducing estate taxes and offering financial benefits to the beneficiaries.

Irrevocable Trust: A trust that cannot be modified or terminated without the beneficiary's permission, providing asset protection benefits for estate planning.

Joint Ownership with Rights of Survivorship: A form of property co-ownership where, upon the death of one owner, the surviving owner(s) automatically inherit the deceased's share.

Joint Will: A single will that is executed by more than one person, typically a married couple, to dispose of their property.

Key Person Insurance: Life insurance taken out by a business on the life of an indispensable employee (key person), where the business is the policy beneficiary.

Last Will and Testament: A legal document that expresses a person's wishes regarding the distribution of their property and the care of any minor children upon their death.

Legacy: Money or property bequeathed to someone in a will or the heritage of physical and intangible assets passed down to heirs.

Liability Protection: Strategies to protect a business owner's personal assets from business-related debts and legal actions.

Life Insurance in Estate Planning: An essential tool that provides a financial safety net for beneficiaries, aids in managing estate taxes, maintains family businesses, and helps to equally distribute wealth among heirs.

Lifetime Gift Tax Exemption: An exemption that allows individuals to give away a certain amount over their lifetime without incurring gift taxes, aligned with the federal estate tax exemption.

Liquidity: The availability of liquid assets to a market or company. Life insurance provides liquidity in an estate for immediate financial needs and obligations after death.

Living Trust: A legal document that places your assets under the management of a trustee for the benefit of chosen beneficiaries, operational during the grantor's lifetime and after death.

Living Will: A written statement detailing a person's desires regarding their medical treatment in circumstances where they are no longer able to express informed consent, especially concerning end-of-life care.

Medical/Healthcare Power of Attorney: Authorizes an agent to make healthcare decisions on behalf of the principal.

Nuncupative Will: An oral will that must be witnessed by others and is allowed only in certain jurisdictions under specific circumstances.

Partial Intestacy: Occurs when a person dies with a will that does not dispose of all of their assets, causing the undistributed assets to be subject to intestate succession laws.

Payable-On-Death (POD) Accounts: Accounts that allow assets to be transferred directly to a named beneficiary upon the account holder's death.

Permanent Life Insurance: Life insurance that covers the policyholder for life, typically includes a cash value component, and pays a death benefit whenever the insured dies.

Policy Owner: The individual or entity that owns a life insurance policy, controls the policy, and is responsible for paying the premiums.

Portability: A provision that allows a surviving spouse to use any unused portion of the deceased spouse's estate tax exemption.

Pour-Over Will: A will that names a living trust as the beneficiary of all or most of the estate, thereby "pouring" the estate into the trust at death.

Power of Attorney (POA): A legal document that allows an individual to appoint another person to make decisions on their behalf.

Premiums: Regular payments made to maintain a life insurance policy, which can be fixed or flexible depending on the type of policy.

Probate: The legal process of validating a will and distributing the deceased's estate under court supervision, which includes paying off debts and transferring assets to heirs.

Required Minimum Distributions (RMDs): The minimum amounts that must be withdrawn annually from certain retirement accounts after reaching a specific age or upon inheriting an account.

Residuary Clause: A clause in a will that disposes of any property not specifically mentioned in the will.

Retirement Accounts: Financial accounts designated for retirement savings, such as IRAs and 401(k)s, which have specific tax treatments when inherited.

Revocable Living Trust: A trust that can be modified or revoked by the grantor at any time during their lifetime, offering flexibility in estate planning.

RUFADAA (Revised Uniform Fiduciary Access to Digital Assets Act): Legislation that allows for the management and distribution of digital assets in line with an individual's estate plan.

SECURE Act: Legislation that altered the rules for inherited retirement accounts, introducing a 10-year rule for non-spouse beneficiaries to fully distribute the inherited account.

Simple Will: A straightforward document that outlines who inherits the testator's property and appoints a guardian for minor children.

Special Needs Trust: A fiduciary arrangement that allows a physically or mentally disabled or chronically ill person to receive income without reducing their eligibility for the public assistance disability benefits they may qualify for.

Special or Limited Power of Attorney: Grants authority for specific tasks within a defined timeframe.

Spendthrift Trust: A trust that protects a beneficiary's inheritance from their potential mismanagement or creditors.

State Estate Taxes: Taxes imposed by some states on estates, often with different exemption thresholds and rates than federal estate taxes.

Step-Up in Basis: A tax provision that adjusts the value of an inherited asset for tax purposes to its market value at the time of the inheritor's death.

Strategic Tax Planning: The process of analyzing and planning financial activities to minimize tax liabilities within the legal framework, essential for business owners in estate planning.

Succession Planning: The strategy of preparing for the transfer of business leadership to ensure continuity and preserve the business's value for estate planning purposes.

Successor Trustee: The person or institution named to manage a trust's assets if the original trustee is unable to do so.

Tangible Assets: Physical items such as real estate, vehicles, and personal property.

Term Life Insurance: A type of life insurance policy that provides coverage for a specified "term" and pays out a benefit only if the insured dies during that term.

Testacy: The condition of having left a valid will at death.

Testamentary Trust Will: A will that creates one or more trusts at the testator's death.

Testamentary Trust: A trust that is established through a will and comes into effect upon the grantor's death, not avoiding probate.

Testator: A person who has made a will or given a legacy.

Transfer-On-Death (TOD) Accounts: Similar to POD, they allow assets like securities and, in some jurisdictions, real estate, to be transferred directly to beneficiaries.

Trust Fund: Assets held within a trust that can include a mix of cash, investments, real estate, and other property types.

Trust Ownership: The practice of a trust owning a life insurance policy, which can keep the death benefit from being subject to estate taxes.

Trust: A fiduciary arrangement where a trustee holds assets on behalf of beneficiaries, potentially offering tax benefits and avoiding probate.

Trustee: An individual, bank, or other entity that holds and administers property or assets for the benefit of a third party.

Universal Life Insurance: A flexible permanent life insurance that allows adjustable premiums death benefits, and savings elements.

Variable Life Insurance: A type of permanent life insurance where the cash value can be invested in various accounts for potential growth.

Whole Life Insurance: A type of permanent life insurance with fixed premiums and death benefits and a cash value that grows at a guaranteed rate.

Will: A legal document expressing an individual's wishes regarding asset distribution and care of minor children after their death.

Made in the USA
Las Vegas, NV
26 September 2024

95819167R00063